1006620981

IELTS

The Complete Guide to Task 1 Writing

with

answers and model essays

Phil Biggerton

IELTS

The Complete Guide to Task 1 Writing

with

answers and model essays

Phil Biggerton

All rights reserved

Copyright © 2010 by Phil Biggerton

No part of this book may be reproduced or transmitted in any form or by any means, electronic or mechanical, including photocopying, recording or by any information storage and retrieval system, without the written permission of the publisher, except where permitted by law.

For further information e-mail the author at:
GodivaBooks@gmail.com or visit: http://GodivaBooks.com

ISBN: 978 0 9566332 0 0

Printed in the United Kingdom

The Author

Phil Biggerton has been teaching English in Europe and Asia since 1992 and in this time has taught Taiwanese, Vietnamese, Japanese, Chinese, Korean, Indonesian, Saudi Arabian, Nepalese, Iranian, Polish, French, German, Turkish, Russian, Kazakh and Spanish students. In the last 10 years he has specialised in IELTS and for the last three years he has taught English for Academic Purposes (EAP) presessional courses at the University of Birmingham in the United Kingdom. He also trained as an IELTS examiner and has worked for the British Council in Taipei, Taiwan as an examiner.

He has been responsible for teaching reading, writing, listening and speaking examination techniques for the IELTS test and preparing new IELTS practice material. In addition, he has also prepared and conducted placement tests for new students and helped to train new IELTS teachers.

In recent years, he has focused on developing English for Academic Purposes (EAP) courses for students who have passed the IELTS test and are waiting to travel abroad to study. The aim of each program is to prepare students for a more intensive learning environment where reading, writing, listening and speaking skills need to be further improved. Study and note taking skills, time management, planning, researching, organising, re-writing, proof-reading paraphrasing, summarising, developing and presenting arguments and the avoidance of plagiarism are some of the aspects that are stressed.

He is now involved in teaching Korean students both general English and IELTS, and proofreading medical papers and case reports for doctors in Taiwan. A new book, **IELTS - The Complete Guide to Reading**, is now in the process of being written.

Acknowledgements

The author and publisher acknowledge the following sources of copyright material and are grateful for the permission granted. While every effort has been made, it has not always been possible to identify the sources of all the material used, or to trace all copyright holders. If any omissions are brought to our notice, we will be happy to include the appropriate acknowledgements on reprinting. The publisher is especially grateful to the following contributors:

p3, Adapted from: http://www.wethepeoplewillnotbechipped.com/main/news.php?readmore=205
p7, Adapted from: http://www.scribd.com/doc/18682197/Cosmetics-Market-Japan-2008
p9, Adapted from:: http://www.wired.com/threatlevel/2008/05/court-approved
p11, Adapted from: http://www.wethepeoplewillnotbechipped.com/main/news.php?readmore=205
p15, Adapted from: http://copaseticflow.blogspot.com/2008/02/british-ufo-sightings-increase.html
p16, Adapted from: *World Energy Outlook* © OECD/IEA,2007, figure 5.2, p. 200
p18, Adapted from: http://www.srgnet.com/pdf/DigitalPlayerVideoUse_07-Q4.pdf
p19, Adapted from: http://wwwdiseaseproof.com/2007/09/articles/hurtful-food/unrefined-plant-food-consumption-vs-the-killer-diseases/
p25, Adapted from: Abu Dhabi Men's College, Higher Diploma Year 1 website/
http://www.admc.hct.ac.ae/hd1/english/graphs/bar_literacy.html /
http://www.unicef.org/sowc04/files/Table5.pdf
p26, Adapted from: Abu Dhabi Men's College, Higher Diploma Year 1 website/
http://www.admc.hct.ac.ae/hd1/english/graphs/bar_accidents2.htm /
http://www.eustatistics.gov.uk/statistics_in_focus/downloads/KS-NZ-03-006-__-N-EN.pdf
p35, http://www.bbc.co.uk/weather/world/city_guides/results.shtml?tt=TT003820/
p39, Adapted from: http://www.census.gov/
p43, Adapted from: *World Energy Outlook* © OECD/IEA, 2006, table 15.2, page 431
p49, Adapted from: http://www.heartstats.org/temp/Dopaspmainspdocspweb06.pdf
Allender S, Peto V, Scarborough P, Boxer A, Rayner M (2006) Diet, physical activity and obesity statistics. British Heart Foundation: London.
p50, Adapted from: http://www.ers.usda.gov/Publications/EIB33/EIB33.pdf
p52, Adapted from: http://www.geocraft.com/WVFossils/greenhouse_data.html
p53, Adapted from: http://answers.vizu.com/solutions/pr/pdf/Global_Warming_Report.pdf
p55, Adapted from: http://www.ch2m.com/nchrp/rural/Section03.htm
60, Adapted from: http://www.prweb.com/releases/2007/01/prweb500303.htm
p63, Adapted from: http://www.frankwbaker.com/mediause.htm
p67, Adapted from: http://www.heartstats.org/temp/Dopaspmainspdocspweb06.pdf
p76, Adapted from: http://www.emt-india.net/process/distillery/Brewery_process.html
p81, Adapted from: http://www.emt-india.net/process/dairy/pdf/CheeseManufacturingProcess.pdf
p82, Adapted from: http://www.royalpuer.com/teafaq.asp
p83, Adapted from: http://www.akashi-tai.com/eng/production.html
p84, Adapted from: http://www1.eere.energy.gov/biomass/abcs_biofuels.html
p85, Adapted from: http://www.mrsvandyke.com/chicks.html
p87, Adapted from: © Sheri Amsel from www.exploringnature.org
p89, Adapted from: http://www.ucmrp.ucdavis.edu/publications/mosquitolifecyclephotopage.html
p90, Designed by Maria Fremlin and illustrated by Carim Nahaboo:
http://maria.fremlin.de/stagbeetles/lifecycle.html
p91, © 2006 Katie R. Roussy, University of Illinois at Urbana-Champaign/Images and photographs courtesy of the National Oceanic and Atmospheric Administration

p92, Adapted from: http://medicalimages.allrefer.com/large/circulation-of-blood-through-the-heart.jpg / http://www.cancerhelp.org.uk/cancer_images/circul.gif
p100, Adapted from: http://www.specialistccs.com/images/process_diag.gif
p101, Adapted from: http://www.mindtools.com/pages/article/newTMC_97.html
p104, Adapted from: http://www.explainthatstuff.com/barcodescanners.html
p105, http://danielliew.com/?s=petronas
p107, Adapted From:
http://www.cnn.com/2010/WORLD/americas/02/27/top10.earthquakes.chile/index.html?hpt=C2 /
http://www.nato.int/multi/interactive-maps/dl_map_en.html#blank
p111, designed by Ali Alqhatany
p113, designed by Ali Alqhatany

The following images are taken from Wikipedia, Wikimedia Commons and Structured Analysis Wiki. Material from these websites are usually in the public domain or licensed under the GNU Free Documentation License or a similar copyleft license. Content can usually be copied, modified, and redistributed so long as the new version grants the same freedoms to others and acknowledges the authors of the article used.

p75, Adapted from:
http://www.yourdon.com/strucanalyis/wiki/index.php?title=Image:Figure94.jpg /
http://www.yourdon.com/strucanalysis/wiki/index.php?title=Image:Figure95.jpg
p94, Adapted from:
http://en.wikipedia.org/wiki/File:Wikipedia_article-creation-2.svg
p95, Adapted from:
http://en.wikipedia.org/wiki/File:LampFlowchart.svg
p105, Adapted from::
http://commons.wikimedia.org/wiki/File:V%C3%BD%C5%A1kov%C3%A9_%C3%BAdaje_Eiffelovky.PNG
Adapted from:
http://danielliew.com/
p108, designed by Ryan Wilson
http://commons.wikimedia.org/w/index.php?title=File:Air_conditioning_unit-en.svg

The structure of this book was developed by Andi Reed and a number of the diagrams used in this book were adapted/designed by him: pp2/3/10/11/15/16/18/22/23/37/50/57/59/60/63/

I also want to take this opportunity to thank Ali Alqhatany for his suggestions and help in designing the map illustrations in Unit Eleven: pp111/113/

My chief designer, Neil Anthony Bomediano, was involved in the formatting of this book and was also responsible for designing the cover and the adaption/design of the following pages: pp9/19/25/26/38/41/44/52/55/66/67/68/71/75/77/81/82/83/84/87/92/94/95/97/98/99/100/101/104 / 105/107/134/

Dedications

This book is the result of the interaction between myself and students over the last ten years. It was with them in mind, and the problems they faced when developing their writing skills, that encouraged me to write this book.

Having always believed that "no book is perfect" I am sure that **IELTS - The Complete Guide to Task 1 Writing** is no exception but I hope that with hard work and dedication to success many other students will benefit from using this book.

As many of my students have now returned from studying abroad with their qualifications they have no need for this book but it is to them that I thank for the inspiration that allowed me to turn the beginnings of an idea into a completed book.

These dedications would not be complete, however, without a mention of other teachers that I have met and worked with during my time in Taiwan and the United Kingdom. In particular, a heartfelt thank you to Gary O'Connor for having faith in my teaching ability and for encouraging the development of my own writing skills. To David Kerr who became a good and trusted friend and who often acted as a sounding board for my thoughts and ideas and, as a result, made life in Taiwan a more rewarding and enjoyable experience. Proofreading, design suggestions and general support and encouragement came from John Ross who made the completion of this book much easier than it would have been if I had been left to complete it alone. Another big thank you must go to Tony Hale for introducing me to EAP and presessional courses. This gave me the chance to not only experience a different style of teaching but also created the opportunity for me to focus more on writing English text books.

Last but not least, a big thank you to Razel for providing an ideal haven for writing, and to my daughter Samantha who has yet to experience the great advantages to be gained by speaking the English language but gives so much unconditional love to us both.

Contents

Unit One – Writing an Introduction

- Diagrams with a time period ... 1
- Using synonyms ... 4
- Rearranging the order of information ... 5
- Adding category names ... 5
- Diagrams with no time period ... 6
- Adding units ... 8

Unit Two – Writing a General Statement

- Diagrams with a time period ... 11
- Vocabulary ... 13
- Grammar ... 13
- Verb tenses ... 13
- Adjectives / Adverbs ... 14
- Diagrams with no time period ... 16
- Managing your time ... 20

Unit Three – Writing the Main Body

- Units ... 21
- Rates ... 25
- Prepositions ... 28

Unit Four – Analysing Diagrams with a Time Period

- Future tense ... 42
- Singular / Plural nouns ... 44
- Modes of transportation ... 44

Contents

Unit Four – Analysing Diagrams with a Time Period

- Male / Female — 46
- Activities — 46
- Age groups — 47

Unit Five – Analysing Diagrams with no Time Period

- Finding more key features — 52
- Percentages and fractions — 52
- Estimating figures — 54
- Surveys — 56
- Copying categories — 57

Unit Six – Analysing Multiple Diagrams

- Introduction — 64
- General Statement — 64
- Main Body — 64

Unit Seven – Processes

- Definition — 71
- Introduction — 71
- General Statement — 72
- Main Body — 72
- Conclusion — 72
- Using the correct writing style — 73
- Understanding the diagram — 74
- Verb selection — 74

Contents

Unit Seven – Processes

- Selecting the correct verb tense — 75
- Developing each stage more fully — 78
- Developing your vocabulary — 79
- Purpose for doing something — 80

Unit Eight – Cycles

- Definition — 85
- Introduction — 85
- General Statement — 85
- Main Body — 86
- Conclusion — 86
- Understanding the diagram — 86
- A flexible writing style — 88

Unit Nine – Flow Charts

- Definition — 93
- Introduction — 93
- General Statement — 93
- Main Body — 93
- Conclusion — 93
- Understanding the diagram — 94
- Symbols — 96
- Oval — 96
- Rectangle — 96
- Diamond — 96

Contents

Unit Nine – Flow Charts
- Parallelogram — **97**

Unit Ten – Objects
- Introduction — **103**
- General Statement — **103**
- Main Body — **103**
- Conclusion — **103**

Unit Eleven – Maps
- Introduction — **109**
- General Statement — **109**
- Verb selection — **109**
- Main Body — **110**

ANSWERS and Model Essays
- Unit One to Unit Eleven — **114 - 139**

Getting Started

When starting to write any type of essay, it is important to ask yourself several questions:

> 1. Who am I writing to?

> 2. What writing style is needed?

> 3. What information do I need to include?

When we think more specifically about IELTS, and writing either Task 1 or Task 2 essays, the obvious answer to the first question is, **"For my teacher or IELTS examiner."** However, it is better to answer, **"For my professor at university."** This helps you to understand that, by studying IELTS, you are also beginning to prepare yourself for your future studies at a university in a foreign country.

Then, knowing that your essay is going to be read by a professor, you have to use a formal/academic style. Do not worry if you are not sure what this means. As you continue to read this book, and do the exercises provided, you will find that your writing style changes and becomes more formal, as well as more academic.

Finally, you need to decide what information you want to put into your essay. Remember, a well-written essay is not just an essay with perfect grammar and spelling. It has to contain information that is relevant to the type of article being written as well. Not enough information, or the wrong type of information in your Task 1 essay, will dramatically lower your chances of getting a good grade in the IELTS examination. However, at university it can mean being handed back your essay and being asked to write it again.

The Complete Guide to Task 1 Writing takes you step by step, from a basic understanding of writing about diagrams like bar charts, lines charts and tables, to a point where you have the necessary skills and confidence to take the IELTS test. It is the intention of this book to provide you with everything you need to know to achieve a high grade in Task 1 writing. It has also been specifically designed to make your journey enjoyable and less frustrating. The page number seen to the right of each exercise heading is the page to turn to to check your answer or see a model essay.

UNIT ONE
Writing an Introduction

Although you might think that bar charts, line charts and tables look very different from one another, they all present information in a similar way. Indeed, it is often possible to display exactly the same information using all three types of chart. The main differences you are likely to see are because some charts have a time period and others do not. Realising these similarities will help you to develop your speed when writing the introduction, the general statement, and when analysing the diagram.

- **Diagrams with a time period**

A typical Task 1 statement looks like this:

WRITING TASK 1

You should spend about 20 minutes on this task.

The diagram below shows time spent watching TV, by age and gender, in the UK in 1995 and 1999.

Summarise the information by selecting and reporting the main features, and make comparisons where relevant.

Write at least 150 words.

It tells you the recommended amount of time needed to write the essay, 20 minutes, and that you need to write at least 150 words. It also gives you the Task 1 statement, or introduction sentence, and instructions on writing the main facts.

Many students rewrite the Task 1 statement by replacing a few words with synonyms but fail to add extra information to the sentence. This often results in an introduction that has copied too much of the original sentence and lacks detail.

By studying both the diagram and the Task 1 statement, it is always possible to write a more detailed introduction than the original. Before writing your introduction, always look for the following six pieces of information, **type of chart, what is being measured, units, categories, years, time period**. This will not only help you to analyse the diagram but also add extra information to your introduction. You might notice that some of these items may already have been listed in the Task 1 statement. If this happens, simply collect the remaining data from the diagram.

The golden rule for Task 1 is not to include opinions for any part of the essay. Never put in your opinions about the diagram and the information it contains. If you add your ideas, for example, about why you think certain changes have happened, you will almost certainly get a lower grade.

Look at Example A, and complete the table by adding the extra six pieces of information.

Unit One – Exercise A   Page 114

WRITING TASK 1

You should spend about 20 minutes on this task.

The diagram below shows information about student attendance in various schools.

Summarise the information by selecting and reporting the main features, and make comparisons where relevant.

Write at least 150 words.

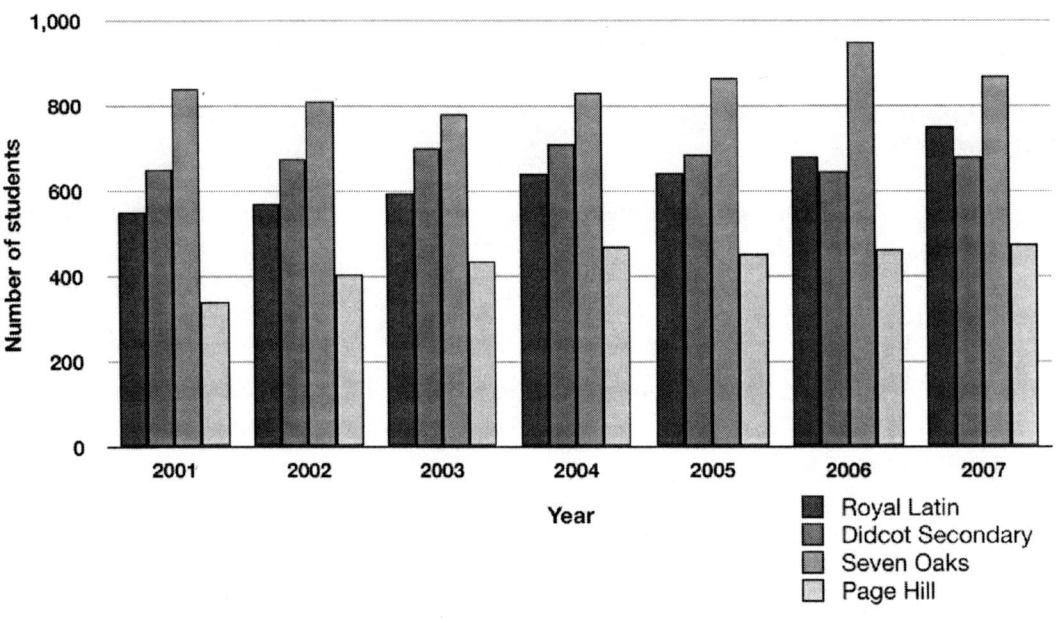

		Extra Information
1	type of chart	
2	what is being measured	
3	units	
4	categories	
5	years	
6	time period	

Look carefully at Example B, collect the 6 pieces of information, and then complete the table.

Unit One – Exercise B Page 114

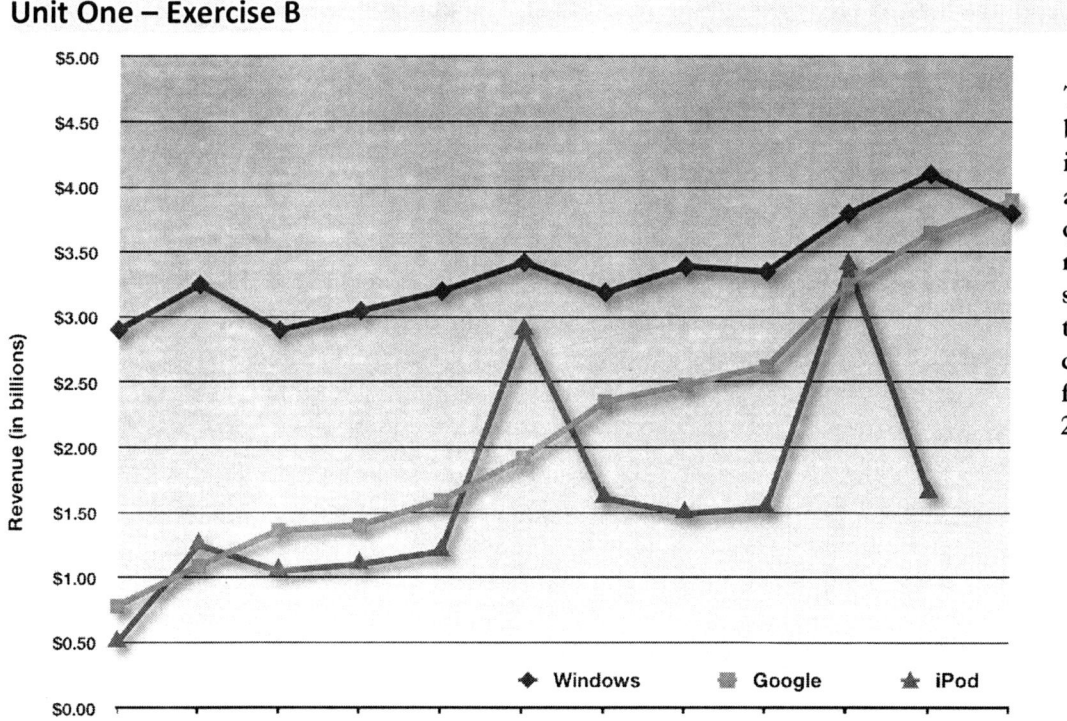

The diagram below shows information about the quarterly revenue of several technology companies from 2004 to 2006.

		Extra Information
1	type of chart	
2	what is being measured	
3	units	
4	categories	
5	years	
6	time period	

By adding this information, you can then start to rewrite the introduction. This will help you to change the original introduction from,

> The diagram below shows information about the quarterly revenue of several technology companies from 2004 to 2006.

> The line chart below shows information about the quarterly revenue of three technology companies over 3 years from 2004 to 2006

3

This introduction is certainly better than the original – it contains more information – but shows little attempt to change the overall structure. The sentence structure, and therefore the level of writing, is rather simple and the length (18 words) is a little short. To improve it, you can use two useful techniques.

- Replacing one word (or a short phrase) for another with the same meaning
- Rearranging the order of some words or phrases.

You may not have to, or be able to, use both methods when rewriting the Task 1 introduction sentence, but it is always good to look for the opportunity to do so. Now look at the Task 1 statement for Example B again. Try to see how the introduction can be improved even more by using synonyms, and rearranging the order of certain phrases.

Using synonyms

Look at the following examples to see how this can be done.

Original phrase:

shows information ➡ **compares and contrasts data on the changes in the amount of**

an important grammar point here is that you will have to decide if you need to use one of the following expressions:

1. **changes in the amount of**   (used for non-count nouns e.g. **money**)
2. **changes in the number of**   (used for count nouns e.g. **students**)
3. **changes in .... levels**   (used for changes in e.g. **population / pollution**)

Original phrase:

several technology companies ➡ **three different hi-tech companies**

you would not write – **the three different hi-tech companies** because by using the article (**the**) we are suggesting that the names of the three companies are already known to the reader.

Original phrase:

2004 to 2006 ➡ **over a three-year period from 2004 to 2006**

Do not write, **shows that / provides data that**, or indeed any phrase that includes the word, **that**. This suggests you are going to provide information explaining what has happened in the diagram. However, this is the purpose of the general statement and main body. The introduction only answers the question, **What is it?**

Also, you do not need to include the word **below**, or a synonym of it, because this would not be true. Remember that you will be writing your essay on the exam paper, and this has no diagram on it. Notice that 2004 to 2006 is a three-year period and not a two-year period. You have data for the whole of 2004, 2005 and 2006. This makes it three years in total.

- Rearranging the order of information

A phrase can often be rearranged, but the original information is kept the same.

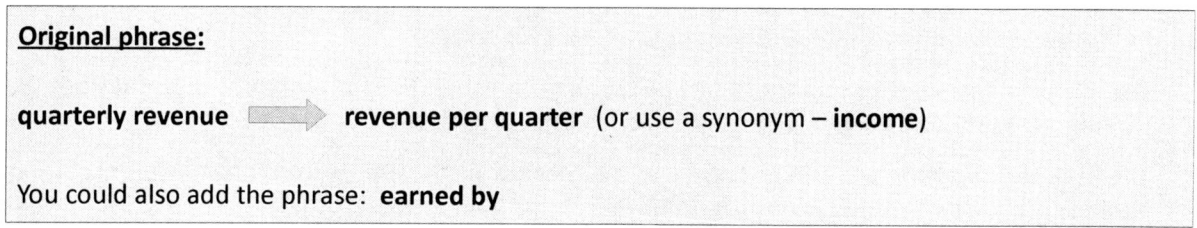

If you now put all of these changes together, you end up with,

The line chart compares and contrasts data, on the changes in the amount of income per quarter, earned by three different hi-tech companies, over a three-year period, from 2004 to 2006.

This is 31 words and just over 20% of your essay.

- **Adding category names**

If you wanted to, you could also list the names of the items, or categories, in the diagram. However, it is not a good idea to add them to this example because the introduction would become too long. Ideally, the combined length of the introduction and general statement is between 50 to 60 words. This means that the introduction can sometimes be a little longer if more information needs to be added. However, the general statement would then need to be a little shorter. A good rule to remember is, do not list the names of the categories if there are more than four of them. For instance, we do not want to have an introduction that looks like this,

The line chart compares and contrasts data on the changes in the population levels of eight different countries, for example, Switzerland, Belgium, France, Germany, Holland, Italy, Greece and Norway over a six-year period from 2001 to 2006.

Also, if you do decide to include the names of each item, make sure that this is done in the correct way.

Look at the following examples and see which sentences list the items correctly. Discuss your answers with a classmate and see if you both agree.

1	The line chart compares and contrasts data on the changes in the GDP levels of three different cities, namely Paris, New York and Tokyo, over a 12-year period from 1996 to 2007.
2	The line chart compares and contrasts data on the changes in the GDP levels of three different cities including, Paris, New York and Tokyo, over a 12-year period from 1996 to 2007.
3	The line chart compares and contrasts data on the changes in the GDP levels of three different cities for instance, Paris, New York and Tokyo, over a 12-year period from 1996 to 2007.
4	The line chart compares and contrasts data on the changes in the GDP levels of three different cities, Paris, New York and Tokyo, over a 12-year period from 1996 to 2007.
5	The line chart compares and contrasts data on the changes in the GDP levels of three different cities like, Paris, New York and Tokyo, over a 12-year period from 1996 to 2007.
6	The line chart compares and contrasts data on the changes in the GDP levels of three different cities such as, Paris, New York and Tokyo, over a 12-year period from 1996 to 2007.
7	The line chart compares and contrasts data on the changes in the GDP levels of three different cities for example, Paris, New York and Tokyo, over a 12-year period from 1996 to 2007.

Only two of these examples are correct. You have to remember that you are listing the names of all of the categories – Paris, New York and Tokyo – and so you cannot write, **including, for instance, like, such as, for example**. These imply that other cities are also in the diagram, and the three you listed are only some of them. In other words, these sentences suggest the three cities are only examples of a longer list. Only **1** and **4** are correct styles for including a list of items in the introduction.

- **Diagrams with no time period**

Although many diagrams have a time period, many do not. This obviously changes what you can write about in each paragraph. An introduction, for example, can no longer state, **compares and contrasts data on the changes in the amount of**. If there is no time period nothing can change. One way of altering this phrase is by writing, **compares and contrasts data on the differences in the amount of**.

Introductions also tend to be shorter, when there is no time period, because there is no need to put in a phrase like, **over a ten-year period from 1996 to 2005**. This might give you more opportunity to list the category names, and still only write between 50 to 60 words for the introduction and general statement. Remember, this should only apply if the lists are up to four items in total. The examiner does not want to see long lists. Alternatively, you could add extra information about the units used in the diagram.

Now look at Example C about the sale of various products in Japan in 2004. Collect the six key pieces of information.

Unit One – Exercise C Page 114

Baby care	24.3
Bath and shower products	195.5
Deodorants	29.3
Hair care	615.5
Contact lens cleaner	627.0
Men's grooming products	174.7
Oral hygiene	212.9
Fragrances	63.1
Skin care	1,427.4
Depilatories	44.6
Sun care	29.6
Cosmetics	3,323.3
(billions of US$)	

		Extra Information
1	type of chart	
2	what is being measured	
3	units	
4	categories	
5	time	
6	time period	

If you have done this correctly, the extra data can now be added to the original Task 1 introduction.

The diagram below shows information about the sale of cosmetics and toiletries in Japan in 2004.

The table below shows information about the sale of 12 cosmetics and toiletries in Japan, in billions of dollars, in 2004.

7

Now try to change the basic, revised sentence by using synonyms and/or rearranging the order of information.

Original phrase:

shows information ➡ compares and contrasts data on the differences between the amount of

There is no time period so you cannot write about **changes in**. However, you can write **differences between**.

Original phrase:

12 cosmetics and toiletries ➡ 12 types of cosmetic and toiletry products

Original phrase:

in billions of dollars ➡ measured in billions of dollars

Having done this, you should be able to write an introduction similar to the following example.

> *The table compares and contrasts data on the differences between 12 types of cosmetic and toiletry products in Japan, measured in billions of dollars, in 2004.*

● Adding units

You do not always have to include the units like, billions of dollars or kilograms in your introduction. This is a decision that you need to make when writing. They were not added in the introduction for Example B because it would have made the sentence too long. However, it is possible to put this information in Example C. The total length then becomes 26 words – an ideal sentence length for the introduction.

Remember, even if the introduction includes the units, the main body must still clearly state what the units are when you put in figures from the diagram.

Now look at Examples D and E and collect extra information from the two diagrams. When you have done this, try and write their introductions by using synonyms, and rearranging the order of information.

Unit One – Exercise D   Page 115

WRITING TASK 1

You should spend about 20 minutes on this task.

> *The diagram below shows information about wire tap authorisations between 1997 and 2007.*
>
> *Summarise the information by selecting and reporting the main features, and make comparisons where relevant.*

Write at least 150 words.

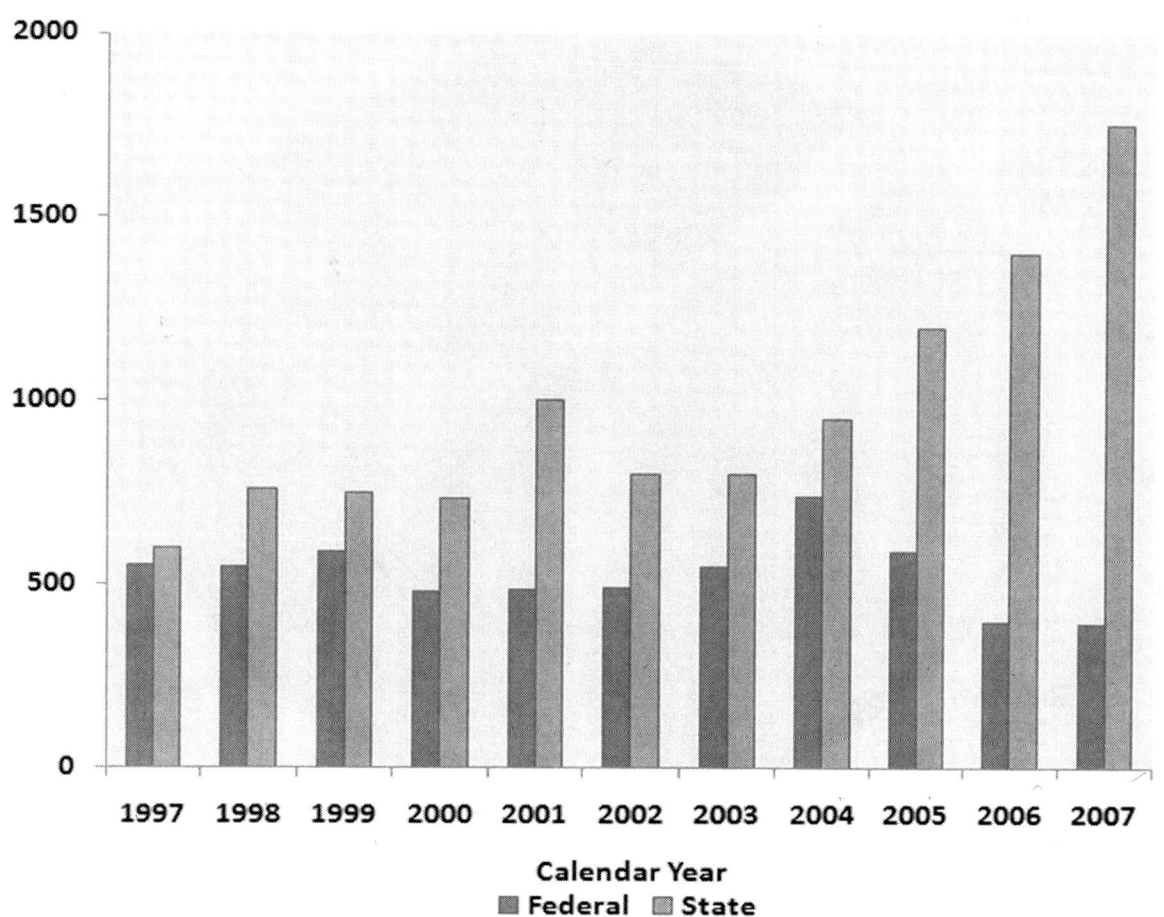

Unit One – Exercise E   Page 116

WRITING TASK 1

You should spend about 20 minutes on this task.

The diagram below gives the results of a survey showing the distribution of foreign ladies wear bought in New York in 2007.

Summarise the information by selecting and reporting the main features, and make comparisons where relevant.

Write at least 150 words.

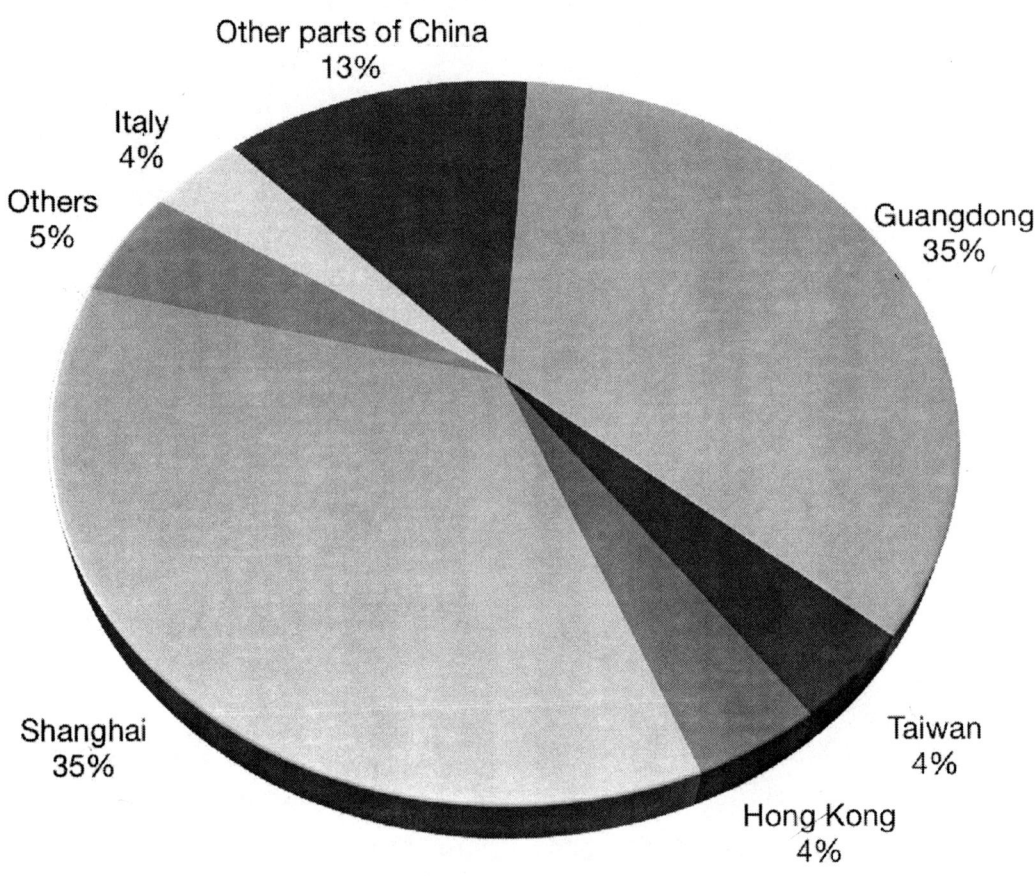

UNIT TWO
Writing a General Statement

The next part of the essay to concentrate on is the general statement. This can be included in the first paragraph directly after the introduction, or put into a separate paragraph. The general statement, as the name suggests, is an overview of the diagram. It must not contain information that is too specific or be too long in length. Although it is a surprise to many, it is perfectly acceptable to have a one sentence paragraph.

As already mentioned in the previous unit, the combined length of the introduction and general statement is between 50 and 60 words. This means that the general statement is usually somewhere between 25 and 30 words in length.

Diagrams with a time period

The mistake a lot of students make, however, is to try to be too accurate in describing what happens in the diagram. This can be seen in the following example:

The number of cars exported to Japan increased over the first three years and then dropped a little but then rose for the next five years and then dropped dramatically for eight years before rising again at the end.

This is far too much information. It is also too long at 39 words. Remember, you are writing an overview of the information. No detailed data should be given, and certainly no figures can ever be included. Although easy to write, there are several different styles that can be used. This depends on whether or not the diagram has a time period.

Unit Two – Exercise A   Page 117

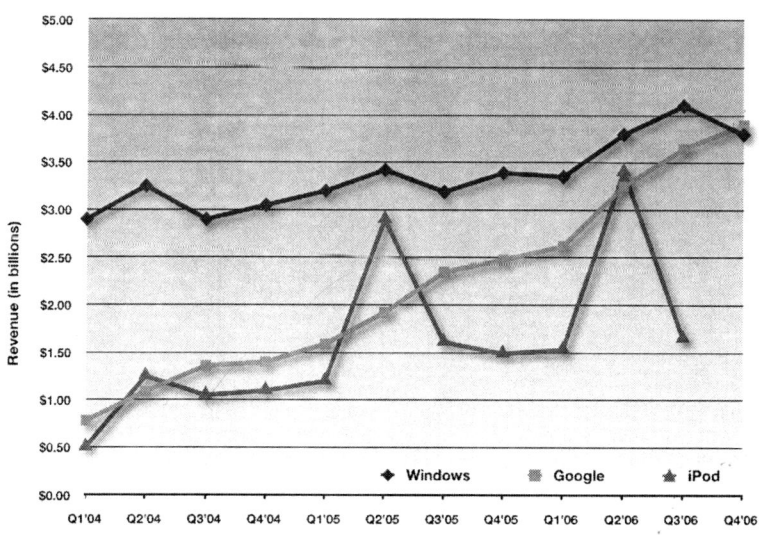

Look at the diagram from Unit One about Windows, Google and iPod again, and try to decide what kind of information can be put into the general statement.

KEY

Windows
Google
iPod

There is usually no need for you to look at any data between the start and the end of the time period. This will make the information too specific for a general statement.

This diagram has three categories – **Windows, Google and iPod** – and, therefore, three trends. Despite obvious fluctuations, if we look at the revenue for each company in the first quarter 2004, and then in the fourth quarter of 2006, we can see that the revenue rose for all three technology companies. The trend is, therefore, increasing for all three categories.

Take a look at the following examples of general statements, and decide which ones you think could be used for this diagram.

1. Generally speaking, the three lines in the diagram fluctuated a lot.
2. It can be clearly seen that, while sales for all categories rose over this time period, figures for Windows were usually higher than the other two.
3. In general, all three categories went up over this time period
4. Revenue for Windows was nearly always higher than the other two categories, Google and iPod, over a three-year period from 2004 to 2006.
5. An overview of this diagram shows that Windows climbed gradually and fell at the end, Google went up dramatically and iPod fluctuated a lot.
6. A closer look at the diagram highlights the fact that the revenue for all three categories, Windows, Google and iPod, rose over this period of time.

Now try to explain why you made the choices you did, and try to suggest ways to improve some of the sentences. Notice the different ways of starting each sentence.

The table below explains which of these six general statement sentences are suitable for an IELTS Task 1 writing essay.

	Yes /No	
1	No	This is too general and you should never use the word, **line / lines**
2	Yes	This is a good general statement showing trends and which category was higher
3	No	This shows a trend but uses the word **UP** which is seen as too informal
4	Yes	This focuses on one category having a higher revenue than the other two
5	No	This is too general
6	Yes	This is a good general statement that explains the trends of each category

Vocabulary

An important vocabulary point to note is that, when writing about trends, certain words are considered more academic than others. For instance, do not use the words **UP** or **DOWN** in any part of your Task 1 essay. They are regarded as too informal. Look at the list of vocabulary given here and put them into the correct column.

Unit Two – Exercise B   Page 118

climbed	diminished	fell	maximised	strengthened
declined	dropped	grew	minimised	surged
decreased	dwindled	increased	plummeted	weakened
developed	enhanced	jumped	rose	

UP ↑	DOWN ↓

Grammar

It is obvious that grammar is a very important part of achieving a higher grade in the IELTS test. However, it is also true to say that your grammar need not be perfect to get a reasonable grade. Although the purpose of this book is not to focus on improving grammar skills, certain grammatical problems must be mentioned.

Verb Tenses

When writing a general statement, both the simple present and simple past verb tenses can be used. However, it is more usual, for diagrams with or without a time period, to use the simple past.

Adjectives / Adverbs

One common mistake, when writing either a general statement or main body sentence, is to use words like **dramatically – dramatic**. Do not think this will help you get a high grade in the test. For example, the sentence, **Generally speaking, the three lines in the diagram fluctuated a lot.**, is descriptive but missing both a trend and figures.

Equally, a sentence in the main body that states, **Sales grew dramatically from US$10,000 in 1987 to US$35,000 in 2007, a climb of US$25,000.**, fails to state why the information is important. So, although the sentence itself is well written, it is still quite descriptive. This can be improved by adding the reason why these particular figures have been quoted. A better sentence, stating the importance of the data, would be,

The biggest overall increase in sales was in Brazil where figures grew dramatically from US$ 10,000 in 1987 to US$ 35,000 in 2007, a climb of US$ 25,000.

Look at these two phrases, and decide if they are correctly written. Then study the tables below.

"____there was a dramatically rise in sales____"
"____sales rose dramatic____"

Increases

Sales	Verb / Adverb		There was a	Adjective / Noun		in sales
Sales	grew climbed rose increased	dramatically considerably significantly steadily slightly	There was a	dramatic considerable significant steady slight	growth climb rise increase	in sales

from US$ .... in 1987 to US$ .... in 2007

Decreases

Sales	Verb / Adverb		There was a	Adjective / Noun		in sales
Sales	fell dropped decreased declined	dramatically considerably significantly steadily slightly	There was a	dramatic considerable significant steady slight	fall drop decrease decline	in sales

from US$ .... in 1987 to US$ .... in 2007

Now look at a few other examples of diagrams with time periods, and write the introductions and general statements for them. Do not forget to collect all of the extra information from the diagram before writing the introduction.

Unit Two – Exercise C Page 118

WRITING TASK 1

You should spend about 20 minutes on this task.

> *The diagram below shows information about UFO sightings in Great Britain from 1997 to 2007.*
>
> *Summarise the information by selecting and reporting the main features, and make comparisons where relevant.*

Write at least 150 words.

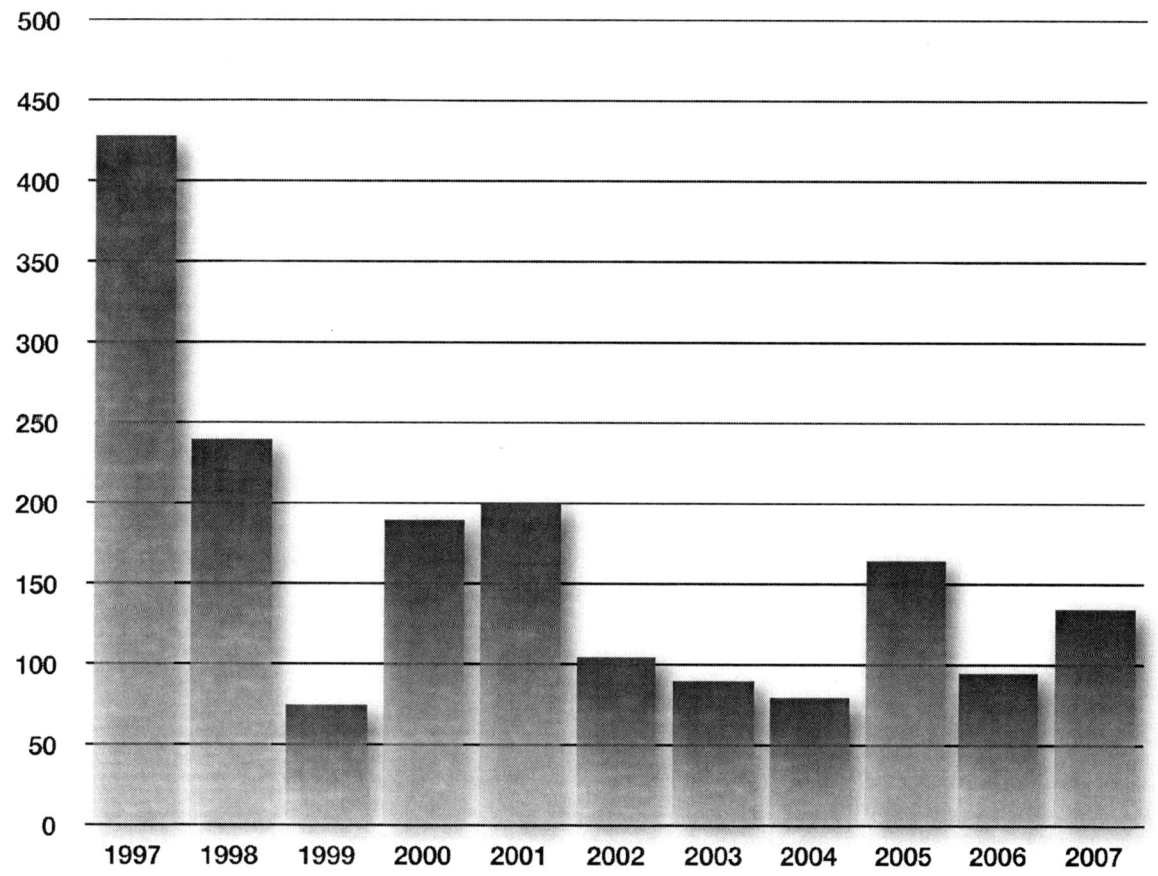

15

Unit Two – Exercise D   Page 118

WRITING TASK 1

You should spend about 20 minutes on this task.

> *The diagram below shows information about the CO2 emissions from energy production in several regions around the world and their ranking from 1985 to 2005.*
>
> *Summarise the information by selecting and reporting the main features, and make comparisons where relevant.*

Write at least 150 words.

| | 1985 | | 1995 | | 2005 | |
	Gt*	rank	Gt*	rank	Gt*	rank
US	5.8	1	6.4	2	6.9	2
China	5.1	2	8.6	1	11.4	1
Russia	1.5	3	1.8	4	2.0	4
Japan	1.2	4	1.3	5	1.2	5
India	1.1	5	1.8	3	3.3	3

*Gt = Gigatonne (1 Gt = 1,000,000,000,000kg)

- **Diagrams with no time period**

As you already know, some diagrams have no time period. This makes it impossible to write about trends because nothing changes. However, a general statement can still be written by referring to the category with the largest figure, and the category with the smallest figure. This is certainly the easiest way of writing a general statement, but you must try not to mention these two important points again when you write the main body. Just imagine writing something like,

> *In general, the city with the largest population was Beijing whereas the city with the smallest population was Berlin.*
>
> *More specifically, the city with the largest population was Beijing with 10.1 million people whereas Berlin had the smallest population with 3.4 million.*

Certainly, it is possible to change the structure of these two sentences and make them look a little less

16

alike. The information, however, would still be the same. This information is important and should really be in the main body, but it now seems rather repetitive. A useful tip is to look at the categories a little more closely and then, if possible, divide them into different groups. This new way of looking at the diagram might lead to a different general statement. For instance, if the diagram looked like this,

City	Population
New York	8.3
Beijing	10.1
London	7.5
Hong Kong	6.9
Berlin	3.4

(measured in millions)

You could then write,

In general, the city with the largest population was in Asia whereas the smallest city was in Europe.

More specifically, Beijing had the largest population with 10.1 million people making it just under three times larger than the smallest city, Berlin with 3.4 million residents.

This has made the general statement quite different from the information that follows in the main body. Notice that the main body sentence has also been written in a different way from the first example. This has been done by including information on how much bigger one city is from the other. Now look at the different categories below and see if you can either,

1. Divide all of the categories into two or three new groups

2. Put a few categories into a new group.

Unit Two – Exercise E   Page 118

Poland	
Canada	
Japan	
America	
Pakistan	
Australia	
Egypt	
America	

With categories that need a good general knowledge of geography, it is important to be careful. If you make a mistake your analysis, and any information you include in your essay, will be wrong. If you are not 100% sure, it is better not to guess. Other possible examples of general statements that use this idea of dividing the original categories into new groups could be,

1. The two most expensive apartments are to be found in Europe, but the cheapest is in Asia.

2. Illiteracy levels are lower in the developing countries but higher in the developed countries.

3. The longest and the shortest railway systems are both in Asia, but the oldest is in Europe.

Look at Examples F and G, and try to write an introduction and general statement.

Unit Two – Exercise F   Page 118

WRITING TASK 1

You should spend about 20 minutes on this task.

> *The diagram below shows the results of a questionnaire showing how many times teenagers in Australia use an iPod in a week to play videos in 2009.*
>
> *Summarise the information by selecting and reporting the main features, and make comparisons where relevant.*

Write at least 150 words.

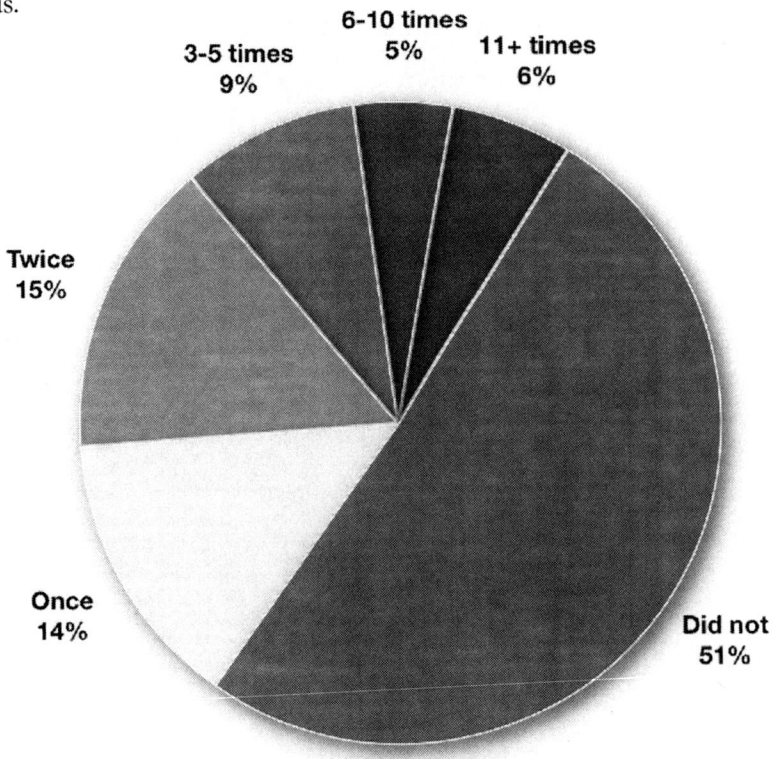

Unit Two – Exercise G Page 119

WRITING TASK 1

You should spend about 20 minutes on this task.

> *The diagram below shows the percentage of deaths from heart disease and cancer, and calories consumed from unrefined foods.*
>
> *Summarise the information by selecting and reporting the main features, and make comparisons where relevant.*

Write at least 150 words.

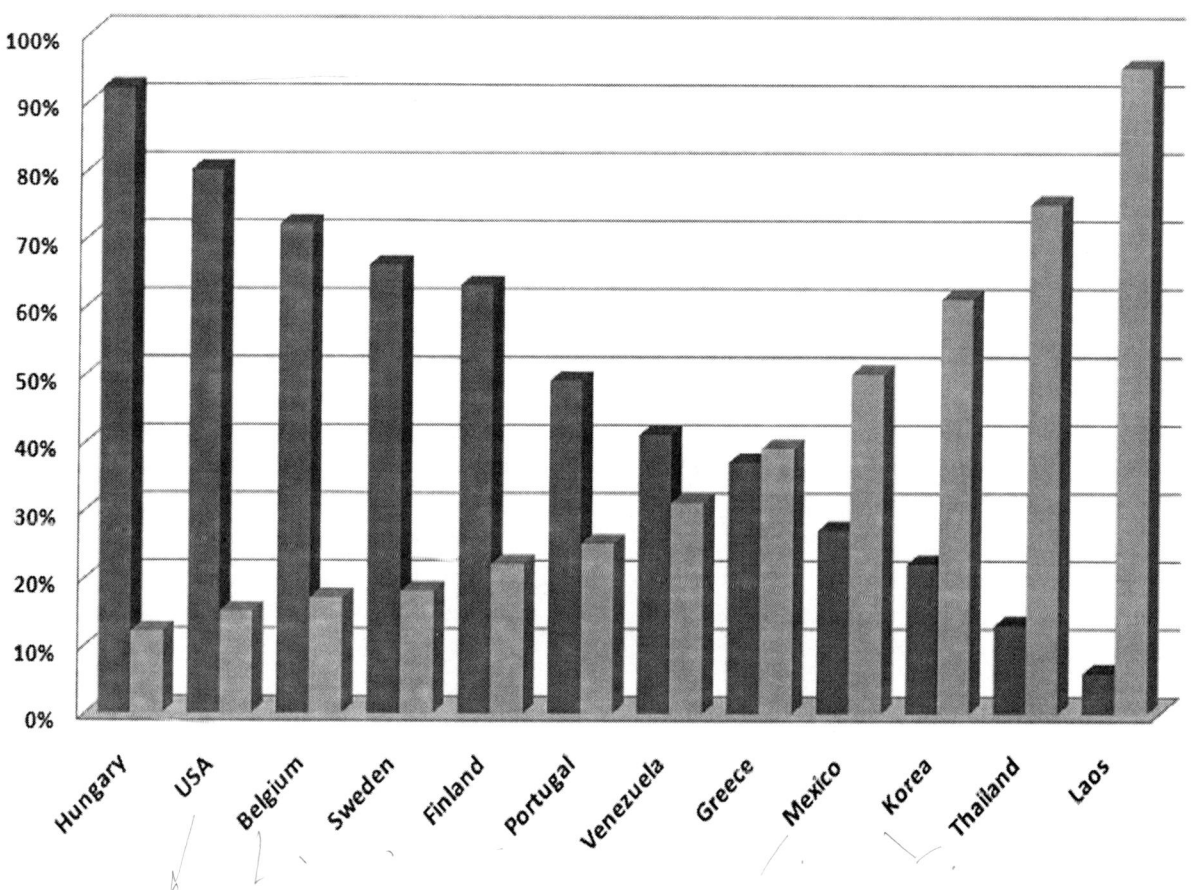

■ Percentage of deaths from heart disease and cancer
■ Percentage of calories from unrefined plant foods

Managing your time

Before moving on to discuss the last and most important paragraph – the main body – it is a good idea to discuss time management.

In the IELTS writing test you have two articles to write and 60 minutes to complete them both. It is suggested that you spend about 20 minutes writing Task 1 (at least 150 words) and about 40 minutes for Task 2 (at least 250 words).

How long has it taken you to write the introductions and general statements in these Task 1 practice tests so far? Do you think you are writing them quickly enough?

Leaving enough time to write the main body is essential. If this part of your essay is unfinished, a very low grade is likely to be given. This means that you must not spend too long in writing the introduction and general statement. Also, if you spend too long writing Task 1, you will not have enough time left to complete Task 2. The following time schedule is suggested.

Number of Words	Time Spent
Introduction: 25 – 30 words	3 minutes
General Statement: 25 – 30 words	2 minutes
Main Body: 90 – 100 words	15 minutes
TOTAL = 150 words	**TOTAL = 20 minutes**

Some people like to write a conclusion, but a general statement is not needed if you do. This is because, for this type of writing, general statements and conclusions are very similar and repetition of information is often difficult to avoid.

Do remember that these are only suggested times to spend on each paragraph. Also, no time allowance has been given for reading the Task 1 instructions, the Task 1 introduction or for looking at the diagram.

It is suggested that you only look for enough information from the diagram to allow you to write the introduction and general statement. Then, move to the main body and start to analyse the diagram. There are always too many important points to mention, so only pick a few key point and then look for them.

In the following unit, you will learn to recognize which parts of a diagram are important and how to turn this information into formal, academic sentences. This will help you get a higher grade in your test.

UNIT THREE
Writing the Main Body

Before you start to write the main body, it is important to make sure that you really understand the diagram. By writing the introduction first you should already know a number of very important things. For example, the table below shows the six main pieces of information to look for before writing the introduction. You often have to look at both the Task 1 and diagram to get this information.

		Extra Information
1	type of chart	pie chart
2	what is being measured	distribution of foreign ladies' wear
3	units	percentages
4	categories	seven areas
5	time	2007
6	time period	(no time period)

By writing the general statement, you will know either,

1. the overall trend of the data, if there is a time period
2. and the largest and smallest figures, if there is no time period.

You are now almost ready to start analysing the diagram. However, it is important to spend a little more time looking at units and what they mean.

Units

You saw in Unit One that it is not necessary to say what the units are in the introduction, but you can include them to make the sentence a little longer. There are certain cases, however, where it is essential to put the units in. These will be explained later in the next section on rates. It is also a good idea to look for units before writing anything because, once you start writing your essay, you might forget to look for them.

Many diagrams use units like, US$, tons, kilometres per hour, cubic meters and percentages, and the numbers you can see in the diagrams are often the actual figures you need to add to your main body. However, it is essential that you always look to see if more information about the units is given. This is usually written close to the diagram but may appear in the introduction given to you. If you fail to notice, problems might occur for the reasons explained here.

If you look at Figure 1, it is obvious that the figures are in US$ where 2 equals US$2, 4 equals US$4 and so on.

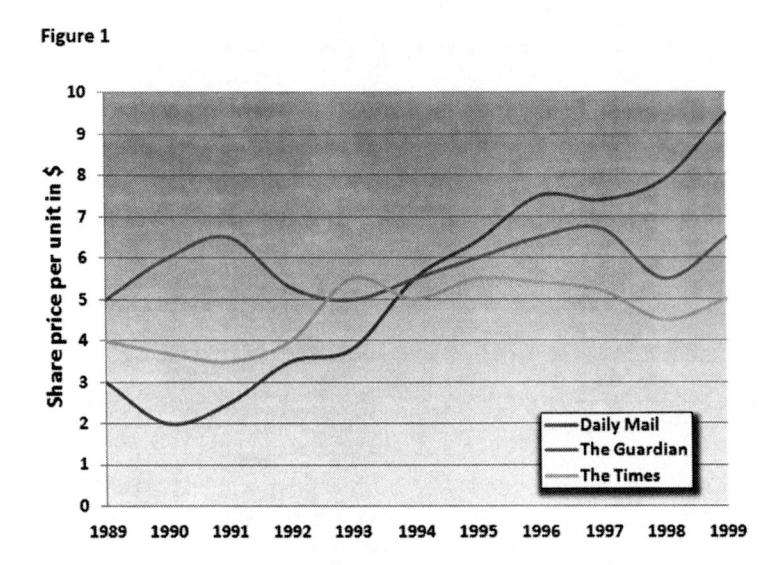

Figure 1

Now look at Figure 2. It appears to be exactly the same as Figure 1, but now 2 equals US$200, 4 equals US$400 and so on.

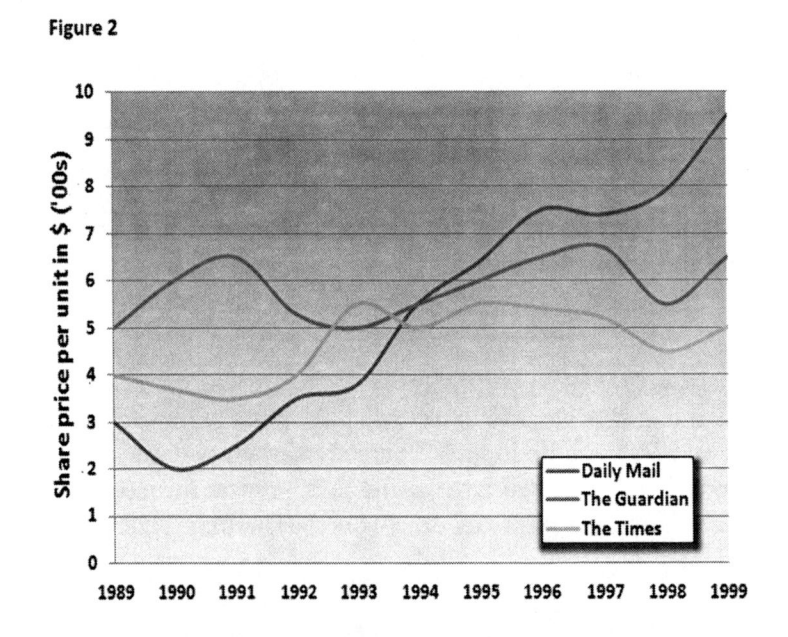

Figure 2

If you don't notice the information telling you that the units are in hundreds, the figures you use from Figure 1 would be exactly the same as from Figure 2. Many students fail to notice what the units and write things like,

> *In 1994 share prices of all three papers were almost identical at slightly over US$5.*

Although this kind of mistake is often caused by carelessness it will, nevertheless, be seen by the examiner as a sign that you do not fully understand the diagram. If all of the figures in your main body are wrong, a lower grade must be expected. There is really no mystery about units. They are used to make the diagram easier to read. Look at the examples below (Figures 3 and 4) and decide which one shows the information more clearly. Why do you think that is?

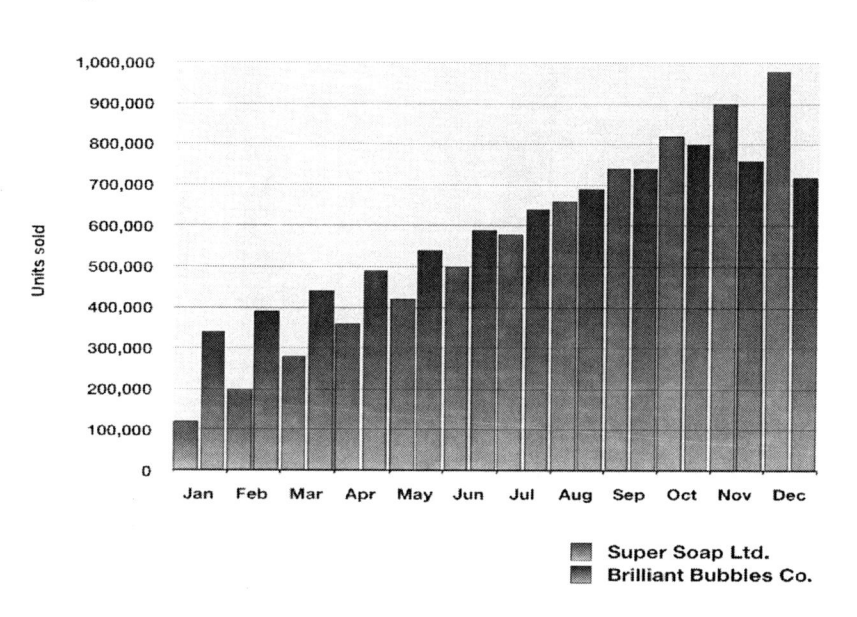

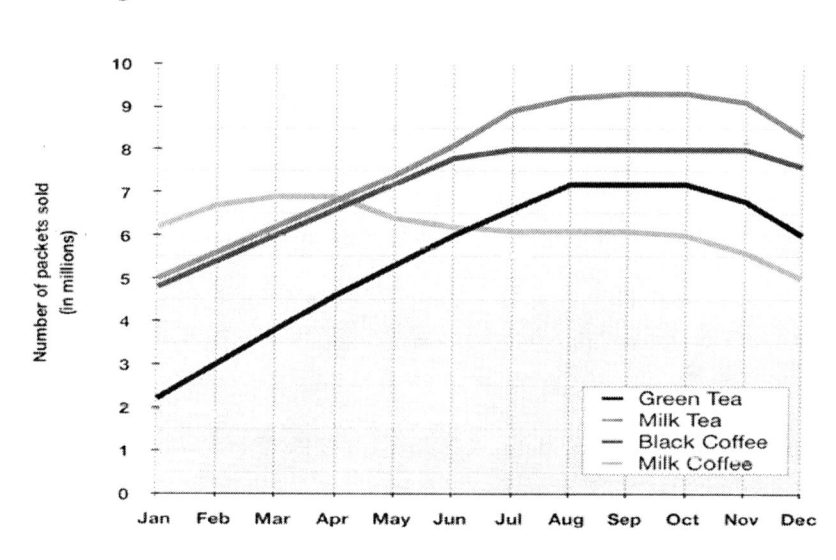

Figure 3.

Figure 4.

Although Figure 3 shows the exact figures, it is more difficult to understand at a glance because each number has so many zeros. Figure 4 is much clearer, but you have to convert the figures you can see into what they really are. For instance, 1 is really 1,000,000 packets and 2 is 2,000,000 packets.

23

Now look at the kind of units that are often seen in a diagram. Write how the number should be written in the main body in the spaces provided. You can write the answers as words or in figures.

Unit Three – Exercise A   Page 119

	UNITS	Figures from a diagram
1	(00's)	6
2	(000's)	3.2
3	in thousands	18
4	units in millions	2.7
5	units in hundreds of pens	16.5

1. e.g. six hundred / 600
2. 3,200
3. 18,000
4. 2,700,000
5. _____

Now look at the example main body sentences below, and try to decide whether they are correct. If not, what do you think might be wrong with them?

Unit Three – Exercise B   Page 119

1. Japan exported five cars to the USA in 1997, the highest figure among all four categories. (units are in millions of cars)

2. The least preferred activity in America was cricket with only six thousands playing this game at high school.

3. Online shoppers bought more books (63.7 millions of books) than any other item.

4. The most expensive four-bedroom houses were in Seattle at an average cost of 2.5 millions of dollars.

24

Rates

Rates indicate how often something happens. They can be written as a percentage, or in terms of its relationship to a fixed predetermined number. For example, *The literacy rate in Egypt for males in 1990 was 60% of the population, or three out of five men.* Now look at Example C about the literacy rates in various countries in 1990 and 2000. Answer the eight questions that follow.

Unit Three – Exercise C   Page 120

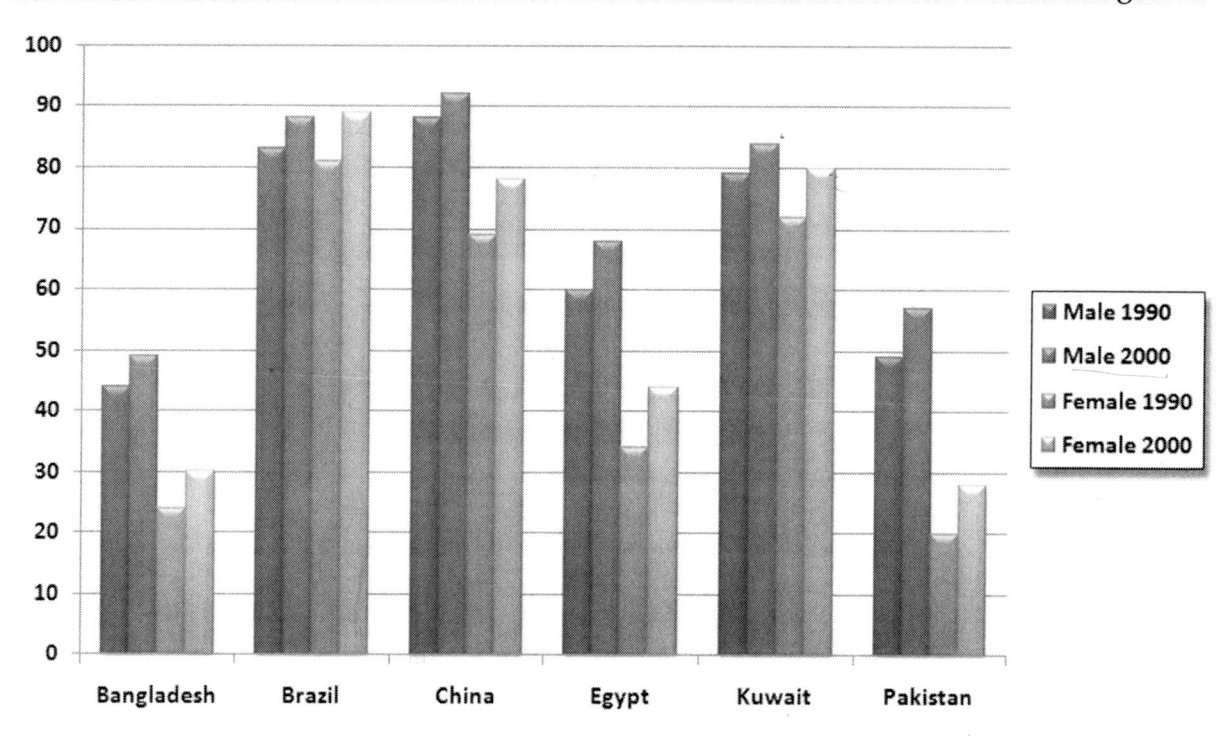

[Bar chart showing literacy rates (Male 1990, Male 2000, Female 1990, Female 2000) for Bangladesh, Brazil, China, Egypt, Kuwait, and Pakistan]

1. Which country had the lowest literacy rate for women in 2000?
2. Which country had a slightly higher literacy rate for women than for men in 2000?
3. What is the general trend for literacy rates for both men and women?
4. What is the general trend for literacy amongst men compared to those for women?
5. Which country had the biggest gap (in percentage terms) between sexes in 1990?
6. Which country had the smallest gap between men and women's literacy rates in 2000?
7. Did Kuwait have more literate men than women in 2000?
8. Did Egypt have more literate women in 2000 than Bangladesh had in the same year?

Why are the answers for **questions 7** and **8** impossible to answer?

25

Now look at Example D and answer the seven questions below.

Unit Three – Exercise D Page 120

Road Accidents, 1997 and 2000

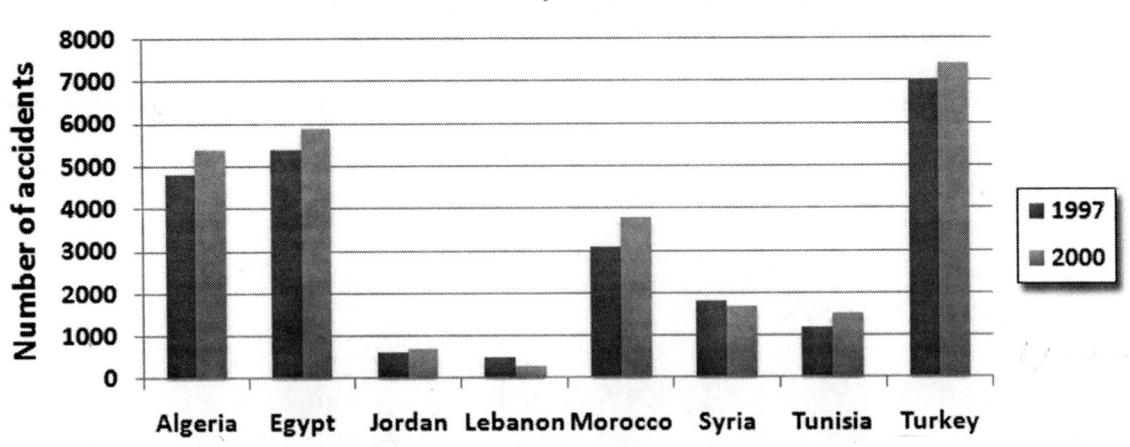

Motor Vehicle Accident Fatalities, per 100,000 people, 2000

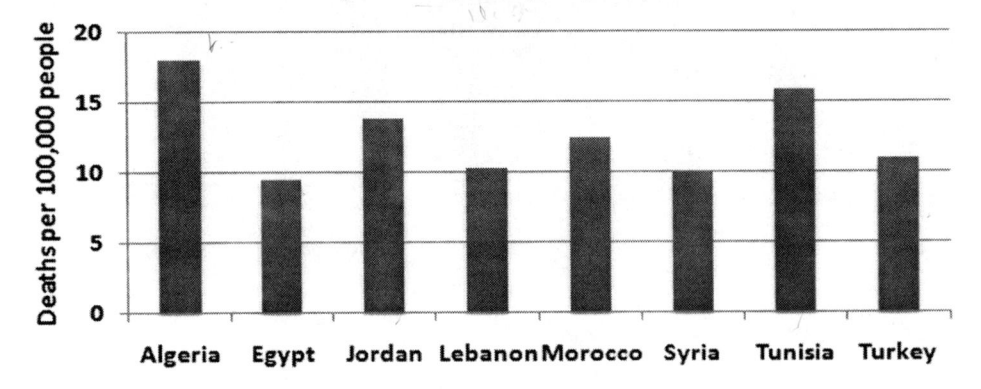

1. Which country had the most accidents in 1997?
2. Which country had the second highest number of accidents in 1997?
3. Which country had the lowest number of accidents in 1997?
4. Which two countries had a decline in accidents between 1997 and 2000?
5. Which country had the highest rate of accidents per capita?
6. Which country was the safest in terms of motor accidents per capita?
7. Compared to Algeria, approximately how much safer was Egypt?

From these two examples, you learn that you cannot state certain facts if you do not have enough data to do so. You cannot, for example, say that Kuwait had more literate men than women in 2000. This is because you do not know the population of Kuwait or the ratio of men to women that live there. Similarly, you cannot say that more people were killed in Algeria than Egypt because you do not know the population of these two countries.

Another important point to discuss is the unit used in the second bar chart, Example D – **the number of deaths per 100,000 people.** If you write a sentence like,

> *The highest number of deaths per 100,000 people was in Algeria with exactly 18 deaths per 100,000 people whereas the lowest number of deaths per 100,000 people was slightly over nine deaths per 100,000 people in Egypt.*

You can see that the unit has been repeated four times. In fact, 21 out of 54 words are used to explain the unit. This is clearly a problem and, units which are too long, cannot be used as much as they would if the units were US$ and %. A good way to avoid this is to include the units in the introduction and then, perhaps, give one example in the main body. After this, you need only refer to the figures used as **the rate** or **figures for** and so on. Try writing the introductions (not forgetting to include the units) and general statements for Examples C and D.

Look at these other examples of how to express rates,

1. infant mortality rate:
The overall infant mortality rate in 2002 for all races was seven per 1,000 live births, which was a slight increase over the previous year.

2. rate of birth:
The Total Fertility Rate (TFR) in the UK reached 1.96 children per woman in 2008, the highest level since 1973. The UK TFR has increased each year since 2001, when it hit a record low of 1.63.

3. suicide rate:
The suicide rate for 18-24-year-old males in the UK has jumped from 58 deaths per million population in 1974 to 170 deaths per million in 1997.

4. fatality rate:
The novice injury rate averages six/1000 parachute jumps (about one injury per 160 jumps) but ranges from five/1000 jumps for men (about one injury per 200 jumps) to 10/1000 jumps for women (about one injury per 100 jumps). The fatality rate may be about two-three/100,000 jumps.

5. murder rate:
The FBI says that in 2006, cities with more than 1,000,000 people had an average increase in their murder rates of 6.7 percent.

- **Prepositions**

Although all grammar mistakes are seen as a problem and can affect the final grade you get, students seem to find prepositions especially difficult to get right. In Task 1, prepositions are commonly used to express ideas like change, direction, quantity, location, time, trends and spatial relationships.

Unit Three – Exercise E   Page 120

Look at the table and try to complete the essay below it by adding prepositions.

	Cleaning	Cooking	Gardening	Shopping	Maintenance / Repairs
Males	0 hours	2 hours	7 hours	3 hours	6 hours
Females	16 hours	18 hours	3 hours	7 hours	0.5 hours

The table compares and contrasts data ………… the differences ………… the amount ………… time spent ………… both sexes, ………… an average week ………… the United Kingdom, ………… five different household activities ………… 2009.

In general, men spent most ………… their time maintaining or repairing things whereas women spent the majority of their time cleaning.

Maintenance and repairs (6 hours) was the most popular household task ………… men whereas it was the least popular activity ………… women; spending only 30 minutes per week ………… this. Similarly, women spent the most amount of time ………… cleaning (16 hours) but men spent none of their time. Men, ………… average, spent five hours gardening which was just ………… double the time spent ………… the same activity ………… women (3 hours). By contrast, the amount of time women spent ………… cooking (18 hours) is exactly nine times more than the time spent ………… men ………… the kitchen. One further point to note is that women spent the same amount ………… time shopping as men did gardening (7 hours).

Understanding how to use prepositions correctly will add greatly to your ability to get a higher grade in your test. Think of prepositions not as separate words, that you always need to decide where to put, but as being linked to different phrases. This saves time and also makes your grammar more accurate.

Use the preposition tables below to help you understand how prepositions are used when writing Task 1 essays. Look at the example phrases that accompany each type of preposition, and try to use them when writing the main body part of your essays.

Prepositions of DIRECTION

TO	pollution levels rose **to** a peak **of** 6 million metric tonnes in 1972

Prepositions of TIME

ON	**on** Monday
AT	**at** noon
	at night
	at midnight
	at 6 o'clock / at 6 p.m.
IN	**in** October
	in 2007
	in spring

Prepositions for PERIODS OF TIME

SINCE	sales had risen **since** 2003
FOR	exports fell **for** three consecutive years
FROM ... TO	**from** 2003 **to** 2009
FROM ... UNTIL	**from** 1998 **until** 2007
DURING	**during** the first half of this decade
WITHIN	sales had risen to become the highest **within** the last 10 years

Prepositions of SPATIAL RELATIONSHIPS

ABOVE	sales in Brazil were always **above** those of the other countries
BELOW	Sales in Argentina were always **below** all other countries from 1996 onwards

Prepositions of POSITION

AT	remained **at**
	peaked **at**
	troughed **at**
IN	**in** Germany
	in Asia
	in all 5 European countries
OVER	sales were just **over** $65,000
UNDER	sales fell by a little **under** $27,000

Prepositions of TRANSPORT

ON	**on** foot
BY	**by** car
	by ship
	by train
	by bus
	by plane
	by bicycle

Prepositions of AMOUNT

BY	sales fell **by** £37,000
	pollution levels rose **by** 62,500 m^3
OF	Japan experienced a decrease **of** £5 million in exports
TO / FROM	sales increased **to** US$35,000 **from** US$18,000
FROM / TO	exports fell **from** £6.3 million **to** £2.7 million

Now complete the following exercise by writing the correct prepositions in the gaps.

Unit Three – Exercise F   Page 121

1. Rises _____ a peak _____ 56,000 tons.

2. With a figure _____ 3,250 kg.

1. Figures increased _____ 670,000 cars _____ 823,000.

2. It remained constant _____ 55.

3. Falling _____ 65 _____ 48.

4. Iran and Libya produce equal quantities of oil _____ slightly less than 70,000 barrels per day per country.

5. People in England spent more _____ travelling than any other country.

6. The number of migrants increased to _____ 600,000.

7. One example is Germany, where the number _____ iPods, _____ 25 per 100 people, is much lower than the number _____ MP3 players, _____ almost 95 per hundred.

8. Italy has the highest figures _____ both categories.

9. Spending _____ food increased the most, rising _____ $85 _____ $128.

10. Illiteracy is more common among women _____ most of the countries.

11. A general look _____ the chart shows distinct changes _____ levels of tourism _____ the biggest growth in Japan.

12. The rate _____ fatalities _____ the road fell _____ 15% _____ 45% _____ 30%.

Summary of Units One, Two and Three

The summaries provided in this book are a way to help you revise more quickly, as well as remember the key points more easily. They are not a substitute for practice. Good grades will only come after you have spent time studying this book and completing the exercises provided for you.

The model essays at the back of the book are provided to give you further examples of how a Task 1 essay can be written. These are not the only way to complete a good essay but will give you some idea of the level you need to reach if you want a high grade in the IELTS test.

Writing an Introduction

	YOU MUST
1.	look for the following six points: - type of chart - categories - what is being measured - time - units - time period
2.	use synonyms to change one word for another with the same meaning, or use a different phrase to replace one word, or short phrase, in order to express the idea more clearly
3.	rearrange the order of information
4.	decide which phrase you need: - on the changes in the amount / number / levels of (time period) - on the differences in the amount / number / levels of (no time period)
5.	remember that **1980 – 1990** is an **eleven-year period** and not a **ten-year period** of time
6.	practice using different standard phrases (**simple present**) in order to develop your writing skill: - presents statistical data on - provides information on - provides data on - presents statistical information on

YOU MUST NOT

1.	copy phrases from the original Task 1 sentence
2.	use the word, **below**
2	use phrases that contain the word **that**
3	use the phrase, **changes in the amount / number / levels of,** if there is no time period
4	list categories if there are more than four in the diagram
5	use the words, **for example, like, such as,** and **including,** to introduce the list of categories
6	include the units if it makes the introduction too long
7	write more than between **25** to **30** words for the introduction

Writing a General Statement

YOU MUST

1.	use the simple past (you can use the simple present when there is no time period)
2.	write about trends for diagrams with time periods – do not rely on words like, **dramatically** or **dramatic,** to make the sentence important
3.	when there is no time period, write about the largest and smallest category / figure
4.	look to see if it is possible to divide the categories into different groups: - divide all of the categories into two or three new groups - divide a few categories into a new group
5.	practice using different standard phrases in order to develop your writing skill: - An overview of the diagram - A closer study of the diagram shows that - An overview of the bar chart - A closer look at the diagram highlights the fact that - In general, - Generally speaking,

YOU MUST NOT	
1.	use the words "UP" or "DOWN"
2.	include information that is too specific
3.	include figures
4.	write more than between 25 to 30 words for the introduction
5.	Spend too long writing either the introduction or general statement. Aim to write both in no more than 5 minutes.

Writing the Main Body

YOU MUST	
1.	look closely at the diagram and make sure you understand the information being shown
2.	look for units
3.	think about which prepositions to use

YOU MUST NOT	
1.	write figures like **15 thousands** or **five millions of cars**
2.	repeat units too often if they are very long like, **the number of deaths per 100,000 people**
3.	state that the actual number of people in one country is higher / lower than in another country when the diagram refers to rates and not the number of people in each country
4.	use opinions

UNIT FOUR
Analysing Diagrams with a Time Period

To learn the skills needed to write a main body takes time and, for many students, are skills that are particularly difficult to develop. However, before looking at what kind of information you should write in the main body, it is better to look at what you should not write. Spend a few minutes looking at the diagram below showing information about the annual temperature and rainfall in York.

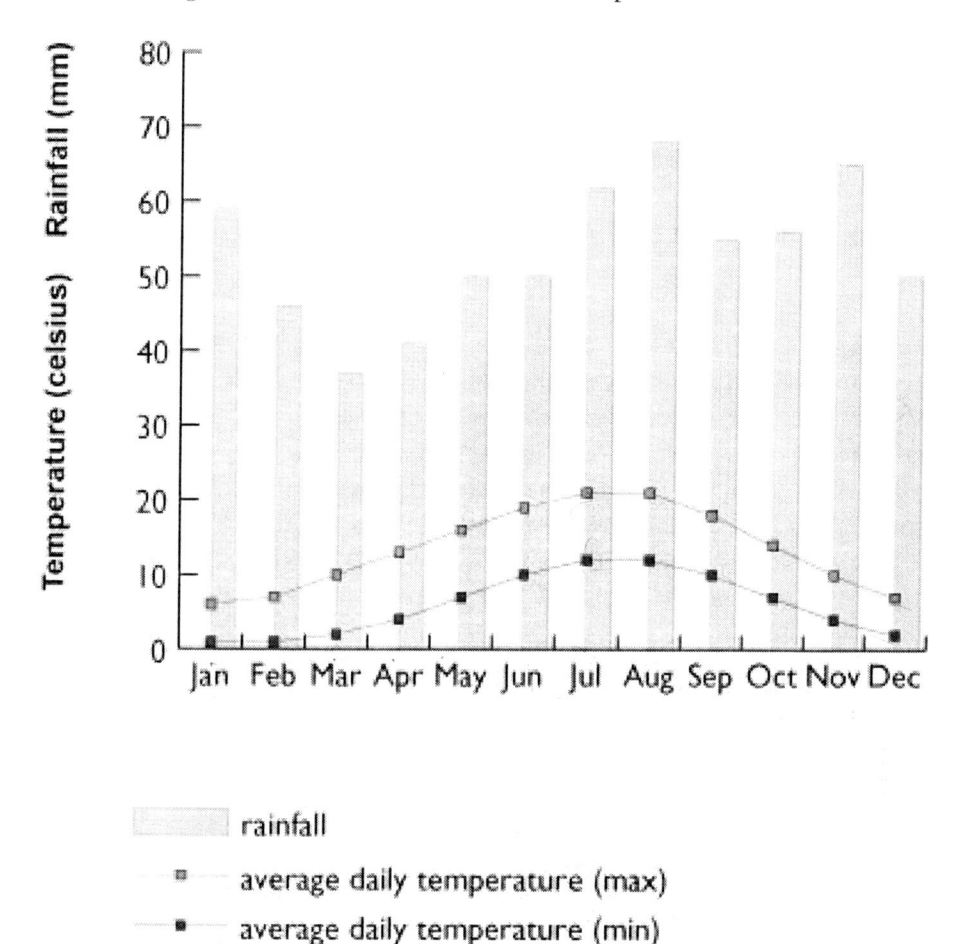

(Chart: Rainfall (mm) and Temperature (celsius) by month, Jan–Dec, for York. Legend: rainfall; average daily temperature (max); average daily temperature (min).)

When you begin to write your essay, you must collect any extra information from the diagram, and use this to write a more complete introduction. For the general statement you can then look for a trend because this particular diagram shows a period of time from January to December.

The main body now needs to be written. To do this you need to spend time trying to select some of the most important features of the diagram. This is where it might seem as if everything is important. If you decide to write about everything in the diagram, a major problem is about to happen.

35

Typically, a student might write something like this,

> The line chart and bar chart provide data on the monthly rainfall and the average daily minimum and maximum temperature records from Jan to Dec in York.
>
> In general, both the hottest and wettest months are in late summer with a fairly consistent temperature range.
>
> More specifically, from Jan to Mar the rainfall decreases and then it increases until May. After this the amount of rain drops a little in Jun but it then rises to a peak in Aug. This is followed by a slight fall in rain in the following month but climbs to a new peak in Nov. Rainfall then falls again in Dec. The temperature starts low in Jan but steadily rises to a peak in the months of July and Aug where the temperature is stable. Subsequently, the temperature continues to fall until Dec. The average minimum and maximum daily temperatures both reflect these changes.

What do you think is wrong with this? Talk to one of your classmates and decide how you would try to improve it.

This is a typical example by a student who finds it very difficult to get more than grade 5.0 or 5.5 in the test. One of the main reasons is that the main body is purely descriptive in form. As such, this essay does not fulfil what the instructions in a Task 1 essay asks for. It states that you must, **select and report the main features, and make comparisons where relevant**. This means you have to pick certain parts of the diagram that are important, and explain why they are important. Another point is that you must always put figures in, but this example has none. Also, references to months have been made by writing – **Jan, Jul, Aug** and so on. Do not use abbreviations for things like days, months and years. A revised version where only certain aspects of the chart are written about could look like this,

> The line chart and bar chart provides data on the monthly rainfall and the average daily minimum and maximum temperature records from January to December in York.
>
> In general, both the hottest and wettest months are in late summer with a fairly consistent temperature range.
>
> More specifically, while the driest month is in May with a downpour of a little under 40mm the wettest month is in August with a reading of just under 70mm. By contrast, the coldest months are in January and December with similar readings of slightly above zero to just over five degrees. The most constant rainfall can be found in May and June when the amount of rain is almost exactly 50mm. Apart from these two months there is a continued increase in the amount of rain falling over six consecutive months from a little below 40mm in March to slightly below 70mm in August.

This revised main body shows the ability to analyse and express the data in a clear, concise manner.

Unit Four – Exercise A   Page 121

Look at the main body example essay on the previous page again, and complete the table below by listing the kind of information that has been put into it.

1.	e.g. driest month
2.	
3.	
4.	
5.	

You can see that there are three key features of this analysis, **the extremes** (driest, wettest, coldest), **the constant** (no change), **the continued rise** (over a period of time).

By using this same approach in analysing a diagram, look for the same key features in Example B and write the main body. For extra practice, you can also write the introduction and general statement.

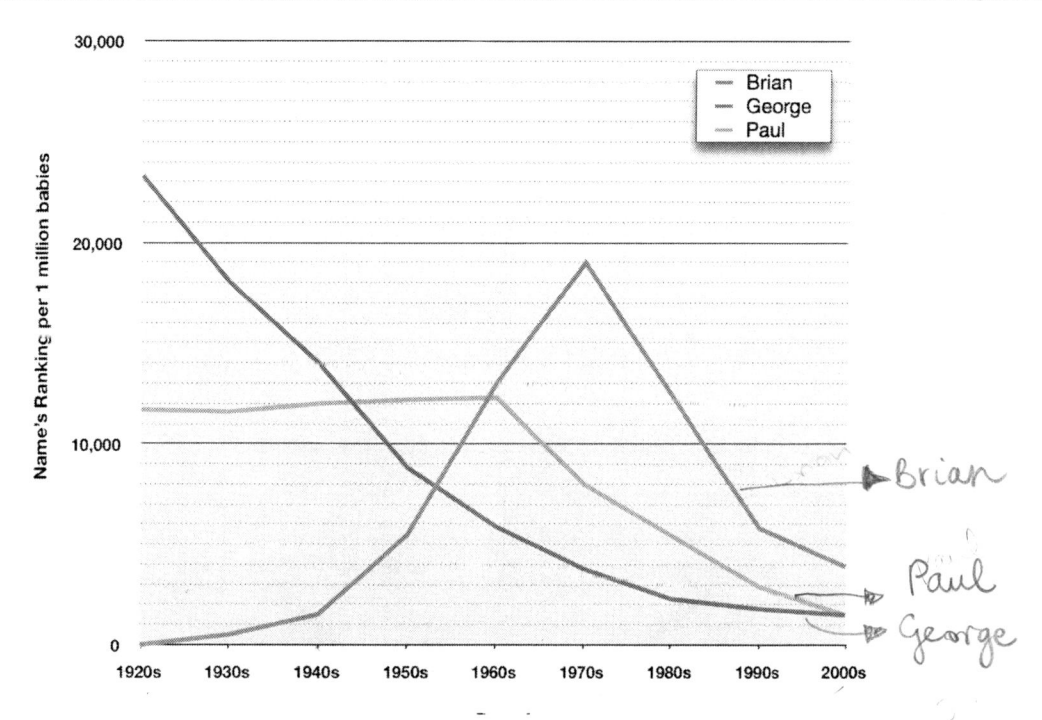

Unit Four – Exercise B   Page 121

In analysing this diagram, the key features found in the first diagram can be looked for again. The following sentences can then be written,

- the extremes

More specifically, although Brian was the least favoured name in the 1920s with very few people opting for this name it was then chosen more than the other two names by the 2000s with 4000 boys per million.

In this particular case, the two extremes (for the beginning and end of the time period) was for one name – Brian. Other charts may show extremes for two different categories, but these are still important and worth writing about.

- the constant

In addition, the rate of parents using the name Paul remained constant at a little over 12,000 throughout the 1950s and 1960s.

It is important to realize that, although the rate is almost constant for forty years, it is only completely constant (no change) for the 1950s and 1960s. A category that is almost constant is not so important.

- the continued rise / fall

The only name to experience a continued fall in usage was George, dropping from the most common name in the 1920s, with just over 23,000 names, to a low of approximately 1,500, a position shared with Paul.

In this example, the key feature is not a continued rise but a continued fall for all eight decades. This is an important analysis because George is the only name to always decrease. If other categories also fell for the whole time period, it would no longer be important. Similarly, if a category is the only category to always rise, it is also important.

- **the peak**

One further point to note is that the prestige of Brian reached a peak of 19,000 in the early 1970s.

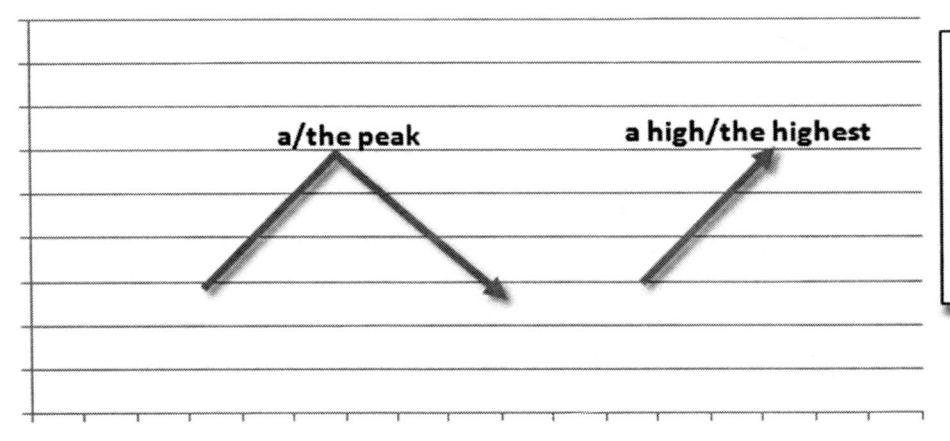

a/the peak   a high/the highest

This is another key feature that can be written about. This is a fixed point on a diagram but must not be mistaken for a point that is just the highest point but not a peak.

➡ **the trough (the opposite of a peak)**

Troughs can also be written about, but both peaks and troughs become less important the more there are. In other words, a peak or trough becomes very important if there is only one in a diagram. If a diagram has, for example, three peaks and two troughs then writing about the highest peak and lowest trough is acceptable. As you continue to discover more features of a diagram, remember that not all key features will appear in every diagram. Enough important data, however, will be there to allow you to write a good essay.

Look at the diagram below about the trend of food consumption in the United States between 1980 and 2000. Decide what extra information should be put in the introduction, and look for trends for the general statement. You have now seen five different key features, and all of these can be found in bar charts, line charts, tables and pie charts if there is a time period. Pie charts can have a time period if there are at least two of them.

Year	Red Meat (pounds)	Poultry (pounds)	Fruits (pounds)	Vegetables (pounds)	Milk (gallons)	Soft Drinks (gallons)	Alcohol (gallons)
1980	126	41	270	337	28	35	28
1990	112	56	272	387	26	46	27
2000	113	67	279	425	21	49	25

This is an example of a standard type of introduction and general statement.

> *The table compares and contrasts data on the changes in the consumption of seven different categories of food and drink in America over a 21-year period from 1980 to 2000.*
>
> *In general, diets in the USA became more fibrous, because greater quantities of fruit and vegetables were eaten, with less protein, alcohol and milk but more soft drinks over a two-decade period.*

This general statement has taken a different approach. It does not simply explain what categories have increased and which ones have decreased. This statement takes into consideration what the actual changes mean in terms of the type of diet people have. More fruit means more fibre. Less meat and poultry means less protein. This is a little more complicated, but it is a nice general statement that shows the examiner you understand the significance of the diagram.

Unit Four – Exercise C Page 122

Now look carefully at the main body, and complete the table by listing the key features used.

The overall consumption of vegetables increased significantly more than any other product by rising from 337 pounds in 1980 to 425 pounds in 2000; an increase of 88 pounds. By contrast, fruit consumption only rose by nine pounds over this time. Although both milk and alcohol were consumed in equal quantities in 1980 with 28 gallons each by the year 2000 more alcohol was drunk (25 gallons) than milk (21 gallons). While the amount of red meat fell by 13 pounds, poultry (a white meat) rose by 26 pounds over the same period of time.

1.	e.g. biggest increase
2.	
3.	
4.	
5.	

All bar charts, line charts, tables and pie charts, with time periods, can be analysed in the same way and for exactly the same key features. However, most people would agree that analysing a bar chart and line chart is easier than analysing a table. This is because bar charts and line charts show increases and/or decreases visually. Tables show changes mathematically.

To avoid possible mistakes when analysing tables, turn every table into a line chart. This is actually a lot easier than it sounds and (with practice) takes seconds to do. Look at the example below to see how it is done. The lines do not have to show how dramatic, or how slight, these changes are because the figures tell us that. The lines are simply to show you what rose, what fell, what stayed the same and where peaks and troughs are.

Year	Red Meat (pounds)	Poultry (pounds)	Fruits (pounds)	Vegetables (pounds)	Milk (gallons)	Soft Drinks (gallons)	Alcohol (gallons)
1980	126	41	270	337	28	35	28
1990	112	56	272	387	26	46	27
2000	113	67	279	425	21	49	25

Now write the introduction, general statement and main body for the following example.

Unit Four – Exercise D Page 122

WRITING TASK 1

You should spend about 20 minutes on this task.

> *The diagram below shows information about the amount of money spent on alcohol and drugs.*
>
> *Summarise the information by selecting and reporting the main features, and make comparisons where relevant.*

Write at least 150 words.

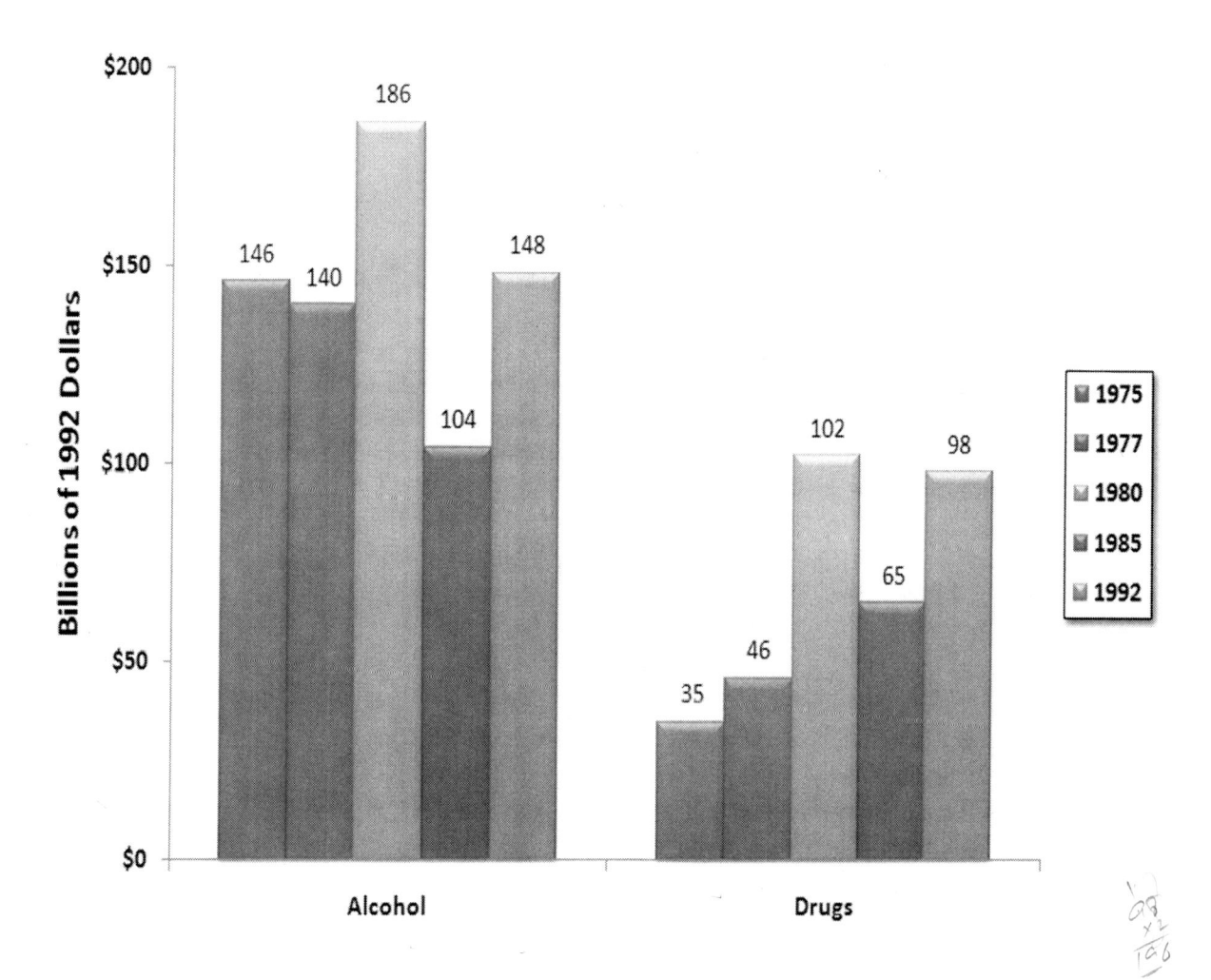

Bar chart showing Billions of 1992 Dollars spent on Alcohol and Drugs for years 1975, 1977, 1980, 1985, 1992.

Alcohol: 146 (1975), 140 (1977), 186 (1980), 104 (1985), 148 (1992)

Drugs: 35 (1975), 46 (1977), 102 (1980), 65 (1985), 98 (1992)

41

● Future Tense

One common mistake made by students is to ignore the fact that some time periods go into the future. This means that you need to use the simple future verb tense – **will increase, is going to increase** – as well as the more usual simple past in the main body. Look at the diagram below and write one main body sentence explaining the information.

The annual production of bio-fuel in Malaysia	
YEARS	Bio-Fuel Production
1995	2.5
2025	35.7

(units in millions of metric tons)

Now check with a classmate to see if you have written the same type of sentence. Did you write a sentence similar to these examples?

The amount of bio-fuel produced in Malaysia will increase from 2.5 million metric tons in 1885 to 35.7 in 2025, a total rise of 35.2 million metric tons.

or

The amount of bio-fuel produced in Malaysia is going to increase from 2.5 million metric tons in 1885 to 35.7 in 2025, a total rise of 35.2 million metric tons.

If you did, then you forgot to take into account that any references to the future are speculative, and any figures quoted are not 100% certain. It is essential, therefore, that you make this point clear in your writing. You can do this by adding words like – **predicted – expected – forecast – anticipated** – to your sentence. You would then write,

The amount of bio-fuel produced in Malaysia is expected to increase from 2.5 million metric tons in 1885 to 35.7 in 2025, a total rise of 35.2 million metric tons.

or

It is anticipated that the amount of bio-fuel produced in Malaysia is going to increase from 2.5 million metric tons in 1885 to 35.7 in 2025, a total rise of 35.2 million metric tons.

As most of the Task 1 examples you will see are only in the past, it is very easy to forget about the future. As a result, many students write the whole of their main body in the simple past and completely ignore the fact that some of the information they are writing about is in the future. This kind of error will definitely lower your grade.

Unit Four – Exercise E   Page 122

WRITING TASK 1

You should spend about 20 minutes on this task.

> *The diagram below shows the changes in population of people who rely on fuel from organic sources from 2004 to 2030.*
>
> *Summarise the information by selecting and reporting the main features, and make comparisons where relevant.*

Write at least 150 words.

(millions)	2004	2015	2030
Sub-Saharan Africa	575	627	720
North Africa	4	5	5
India	740	777	782
China	480	453	394
Indonesia	156	171	180
Rest of Asia	489	521	561
Brazil	23	26	27
Rest of Latin America	60	60	58
TOTAL	2,528	2,640	2,727

Singular / Plural nouns

One grammatical error that can easily occur is when it relates to the use of singular and plural nouns. The singular form of a noun might be used in the diagram, but in the essay the plural form should often be used. This can happen because information, in diagrams, does not always obey the same grammar rules that complete sentences have to follow. You need to be quite careful in trying to prevent this from happening. There are various nouns that this can happen to, but different modes of transportation and the words, **male** and **female**, are among the most common.

Modes of Transportation

To begin with, let's look at different modes of transportation. The example below helps to highlight the fact that, information may need to be changed in some way before using it in the essay. Unless this is done, grammatical errors are likely to occur. After looking at the chart, write an introduction and general statement.

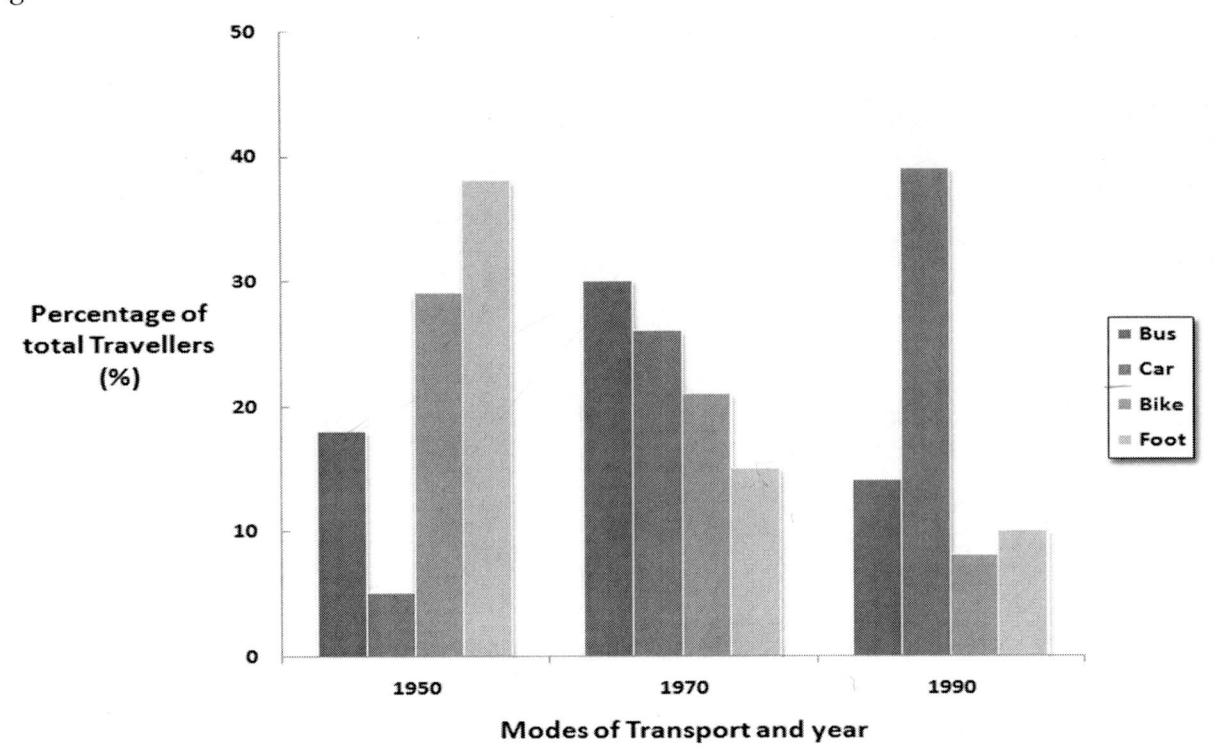

Now look at the following examples of an introduction and general statement for this diagram.

The bar chart compares and contrasts data on the changes in travelling preferences for four different types of transport; bus, car, bike and foot over a 41-year period from 1950 to 1990.

In general, the number of people using all modes of transport decreased with the notable exception of car which experienced a dramatic rise in users over the same period of time.

Both paragraphs need to be changed a little to make them grammatically correct. Look at the revised paragraphs, and see if you can understand why the changes were made.

The bar chart compares and contrasts data on the changes in travelling preferences for 4 different types of transport; buses, cars, bikes and walking over a 41-year period from 1950 to 1990.

We do not say **foots** or **feet**! However, we could say **on foot**.

In general, the number of people using all modes of transport decreased with the notable exception of the car which experienced a dramatic rise in users over the same period of time.

Here we can say, **the car** or **cars**. By writing, **the car**, we refer to cars in general and not one specific car. It is the same as saying, **The elephant is a very large mammal that lives in Africa and Asia.** This is not referring to one particular elephant but elephants in general. If we write, **cars**, we are talking about all cars.

Unit Four – Exercise F   Page 123

Look at some typical sentences that can be written for the main body. Complete them using words from the box below.

1. *The biggest overall decrease in preference was _____, falling from a little under 40% to slightly under ten %.*

2. *The biggest overall increase was _____, climbing from slightly over five % in 1950 to a little under 40% in 1990.*

3. *The smallest range in type of transport chosen in any one year was 1970 when travelling _____ at exactly 30% and _____ at just over 15%.*

4. *Travelling _____ in 1970 (just below 20%) was almost exactly the same as the percentage of people travelling _____ in 1990.*

on the bus	by bus	walking	on the foot	on the car
bus	on buses	by walking	car	by car
buses	on foot	by foot	cars	the car

45

Male – Female

Another type of diagram that can cause problems in using singular/plural nouns is when it refers to information about men and women. This could be the results of a survey into preferred leisure activities of each sex, literacy levels in different countries, average life expectancy in different regions and so on. Many students simply follow the wording presented in the diagram. This often uses only the singular form **male, female** and not the plural forms. As a result, students often end up writing sentences like,

Both male and female spend most of their free time in socializing with friends.

The most obvious trend is that male has a lower literacy rate than the female in all five countries.

Remember that all of these types of diagrams present information about more than one man or woman, so you must use the plural forms. For some diagrams, it is possible to use expressions like – **female students, male students, female readers, male readers** and so on. However, you can never write things like – **women student** or **women reader**. You would have to write phrases like – **only 30% of the women read comic books**. If you say, **only 30% of women read comic books**, you are talking about women all over the world and not just those in the survey.

How many synonyms / phrases can you think of that can be used instead of using, **men** and **women**?

Unit Four – Exercise G Page 123

Male	Female
1. _____	1. _____
2. _____	2. _____
3. _____	3. _____
4. _____	4. _____
5. _____	5. _____

Activities

It is also quite common for diagrams to show information regarding the various leisure activities that people enjoy doing. Students will often use phrases like – **boys like to play baseball / girls like to play netball**. These are accurate phrases but if overused become rather repetitive and boring. Other phrases that can be used instead are,

boys like to participate in baseball	football is the favourite pastime pursuit
girls like to take part in hockey	meditation is the least favoured leisure time activity

Look at the table below showing information about the various leisure activities done by men and women of different ages.

Unit Four – Exercise H   Page 123

Age Groups	21 – 35	21 – 35	36 – 45	36 – 45	46 +	46 +
Sex	male	female	male	female	male	female
Jogging	35%	23%	48%	31%	22%	31%
Baseball	87%	2%	64%	1%	29%	0%
Basketball	97%	22%	68%	15%	43%	3%
Football	78%	9%	57%	5%	27%	0%
Meditation	0%	7%	3%	12%	7%	42%
Fishing	12%	1%	32%	0%	45%	0%

Remember, even though there is no time period here, the general statement can still focus on trends because there are three different age groups. You could write,

> *Generally speaking, the trend shows that participation in all activities decreased with age with the exception of meditation for both males and females and jogging and fishing for females and males respectively.*

The problem here is that it is a little too long at 34 words. This may not be such a problem if your introduction is between 20 to 25 words, but there is no guarantee that it will be.

Remember, we are trying to end up with about 100 words left for the main body, so the total number of words used for the introduction and general statement should be between 50 to 60 words. Try and divide the categories into different groups, and use this information to write a more concise general statement. When you have done this write the main body.

Age Groups

In the same way that using only the words, **men** and **women**, was too repetitive, the style of writing used to introduce each age group can also be rather too simple, and lacking in alternative phrases. Students very often write phrases like,

1. the 21-35 age group
2. the 36 to 45 age group
3. the 46-55 age group

As you can see, this is rather repetitive and shows little skill in expressing the same type of information in different ways. This needs to be addressed if higher grades are to be gained in your test.

Unit Four – Exercise I Page 123

Look at the different age groups taken from a typical diagram, and try to think of as many ways as possible of writing phrases about these different age groups. Some of them have been done for you.

21 – 35	36 – 45	46 – 55	56 – 65	66 plus

1	the 21 to 35 age group
2	the youngest age group
3	the 21 to 35-year-olds
4	
5	
6	
7	
8	
9	
10	

Unit Four – Exercise J

WRITING TASK 1

You should spend about 20 minutes on this task.

The diagram below shows time spent watching TV by age and gender in the UK in 1995 and 1999.

Summarise the information by selecting and reporting the main features, and make comparisons where relevant.

Write at least 150 words.

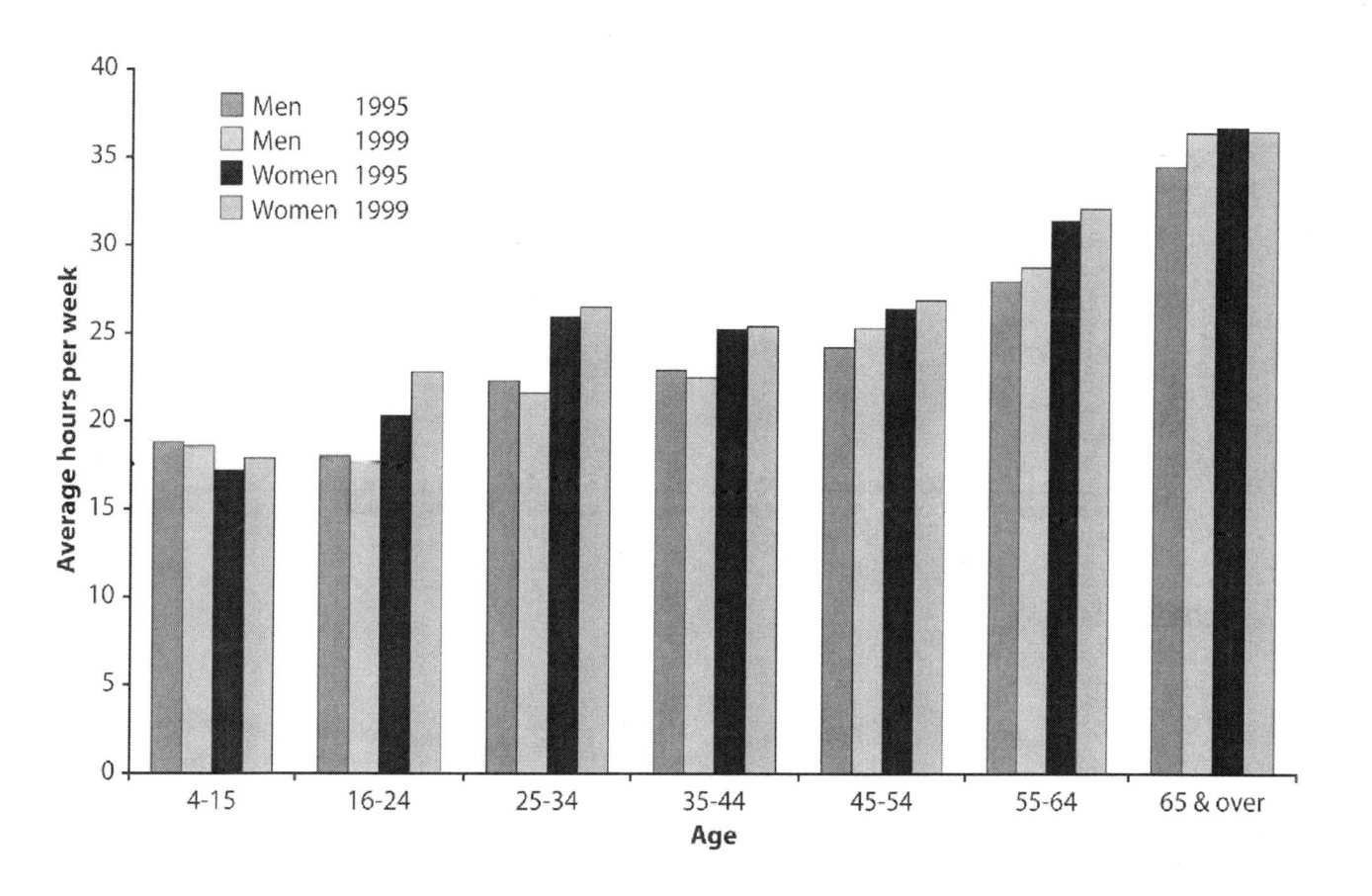

Unit Four – Exercise K   Page 124

The next exercise gives you a chance to see how a one category line chart (**Pork**) becomes more and more complex as it becomes a two category chart (**Pork and Chicken**), then a three category chart (**Pork, Chicken and Beef**). Write the introduction, general statement and main body for each. Diagram One will be more descriptive in form, but it is still possible to compare and contrast because of the time period. Diagrams Two and Three will need to be analysed more to find the best contrasts and comparisons. Also, can you think of a number of different synonyms for, **pounds per capita**?

Diagram One

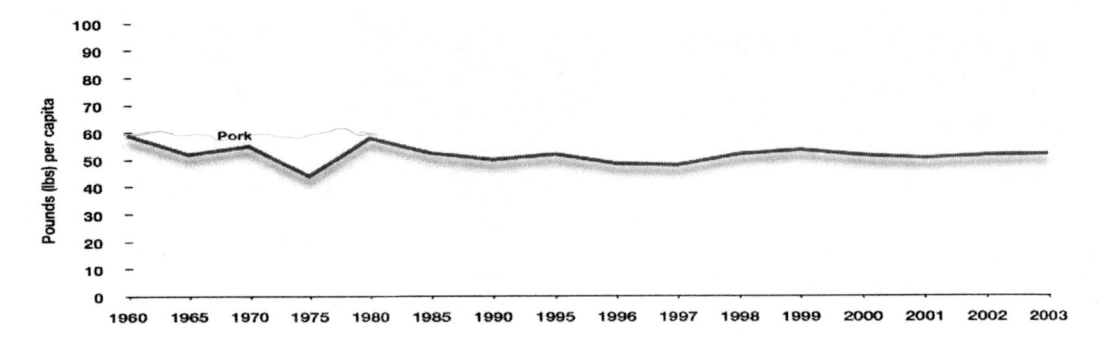

Diagram Two

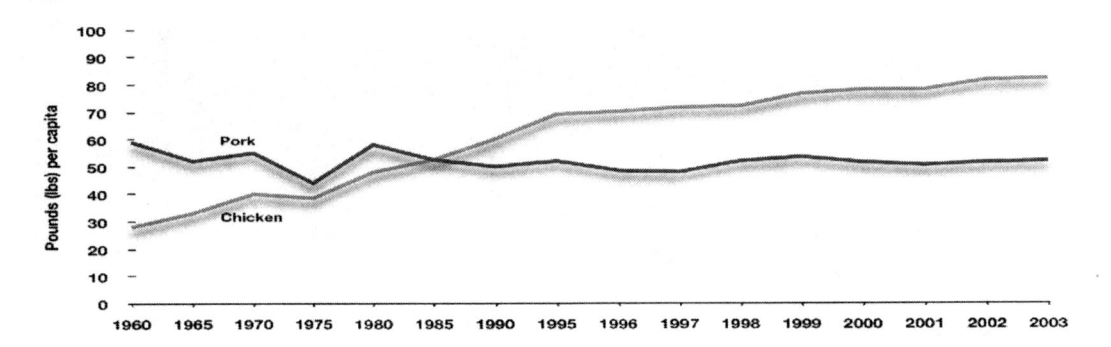

Diagram Three

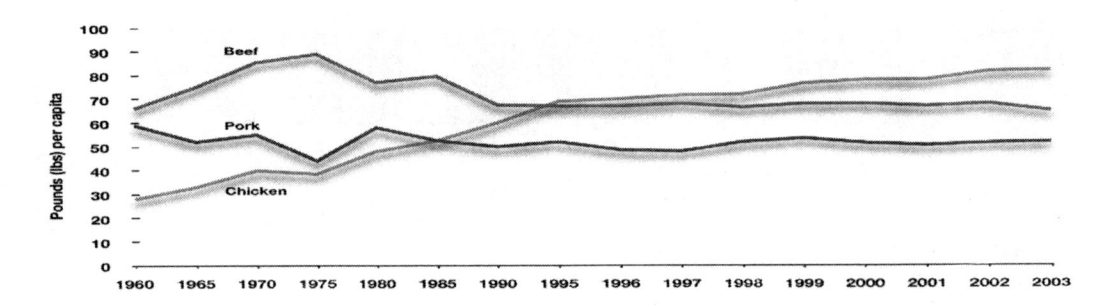

50

UNIT FIVE
Analysing Diagrams with No Time Period

From the previous unit on analysing diagrams with a time period, you saw that there are many different key features to look for. How many of them can you remember? Complete Example A below to review this.

Unit Five – Exercise A Page 125

	Key Features – diagrams with time periods	Can be looked for in a diagram with <u>NO</u> time period (Write YES or NO)
1		
2		
3		
4		
5		
6		
7		
8		
9		
10		
11		

Now that you have done this, complete the final column in the table showing which key features can still be looked for in a diagram with no time period. Having completed the table, you should now be able to see that you lose many of these key features when analysing a diagram with no time period. In fact, all that you are left with are,

- **the extremes**
- **two categories the same**

This means that we have to find new ways to analyse, and further develop, information from diagrams with no time period. For instance, if you have a diagram with percentages it is a good idea to use fractions.

- **Finding more key features**

Unit Five – Exercise B   Page 126

Contributions to the "Greenhouse Effect"

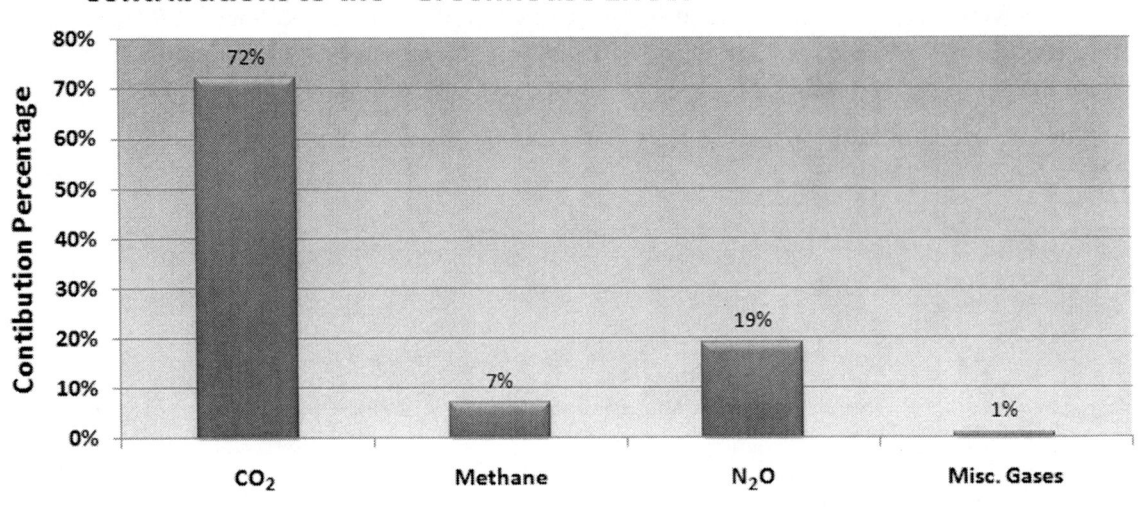

- CO_2: 72%
- Methane: 7%
- N_2O: 19%
- Misc. Gases: 1%

(Y-axis: Contribution Percentage, 0% to 80%)

There are only four categories in this diagram, but it is still possible to write more than 150 words. Possible ways to do this are,

1	Use fractions as well as percentages
2	Compare and contrast the relative size of one category with another
3	Compare the rankings of one category to another
4	Compare parts of a whole (only possible when working with a total of 100 percent)
5	Include figures explaining how much bigger/smaller one category is relative to another
6	Include two categories the same

These ideas can help you use phrases like,

the biggest contributor to	the third most important category
by almost a fifth (18%)	figures of 72.369% and 7.199% respectively
nearly three times bigger	the second main contributor
over ten-fold larger	this contrasts markedly
a difference of over 70%	with much lower figures

Try to see how you can use these phrases in your essay. Then write the introduction, general statement and main body for Example B. You can, but don't have to, use all of these phrases.

Unit Five – Exercise C

Now look at a similar diagram with five categories related to the results of a questionnaire regarding typically held views about the causes of global warming. Try to analyse it in a similar way to the previous example. Then write the 150-word essay using some of the ideas suggested earlier.

What is the cause of global warming?	
26.4%	Human behaviour
25.60%	Natural climate cycles
25.2%	Both human and natural causes
18.4%	I don't believe it's happening
4.4%	Unsure of the cause

Percentages and Fractions

As stated earlier, percentages are often used in diagrams and can be used in line charts, bar charts, tables and pie charts. As you will see, it also gives you a very good way of developing one idea into a more complex sentence. This makes it much easier to complete a 150-word essay. Although percentages are easy to use, you must remember that the word, **percentage**, cannot be used with figures. Do not write things like,

*The biggest overall increase in sales was in China, rising from 15 **percentage** in 2001 to 37 **percentage** in 2007.*

You must write,

*The biggest overall increase in sales was in China, rising from 15 **percent** in 2001 to 37 **percent** in 2007.*

The word – **percentage** – can, however, be used for sentences like:,

*The **percentage** increase in sales was the highest overall in China, rising from 15% in 2001 to 37% in 2007, just over a two-fold increase.*

You can also use the symbol – % – but you must not use both styles in the same essay. When you write an essay it must be consistent. This also applies to spelling. Do not mix American and British spelling in the same text.

Whenever you are writing about a diagram that shows its figures in the form of percentages, try to use both percentages and fractions in your essay. This shows the examiner that you can be more flexible when expressing figures.

Look at the table below showing the different percentage/fraction relationships. Usually you will write only the percentage or fractions (not ½, ¼, ¾ and so on.).

Percentage	Fractions	Percentage	Fractions
	THIRDS		**TENTHS**
33%	a third / one third	10%	a tenth / one tenth
66%	two thirds	20%	two tenths
		30%	three tenths
	QUARTERS	40%	four tenths
25%	a quarter / one quarter	50%	a half / one half / half
50%	a half / one half / half	60%	six tenths
75%	three quarters	70%	seven tenths
		80%	eight tenths
	FIFTHS	90%	nine tenths
20%	a fifth / one fifth		
40%	two fifths		
60%	three fifths		
80%	four fifths		

Estimating Figures

Although tables and pie charts always show the exact figures, line charts and bar charts might not. As explained here, you need to estimate (not guess) the figures that you need with useful phrases like,

> slightly over / slightly under
> a little more / a little less than
> just over / just under

These expressions can help produce a more accurate report of the diagram by combining them with fractions like – **approximately half** – **a little over three quarters** – **slightly less than three fifths** – and so on.

Look at the sentences below showing how fractions can be incorporated into your writing style.

1. In the 1980s, approximately *__half__* of all purchases of watches were made by females (47%).

2. More specifically, exactly *__a third__* of students studied mathematics whereas the other *__two thirds__* preferred to study science.

3. A little over *__three quarters__* of all the people (77%) stated that "Job Satisfaction" was the most important factor that influenced their performance at work.

4. Whereas exactly *__a fifth__* of the inhabitants had decided not to vote, slightly less than *__three fifths__* of all citizens in Buckingham (58%) cast their decision on that day.

5. Although Coca-Cola's market share remained stable during this period, the proportion of Pepsi's rose to account for precisely *__three tenths__* of the total.

Notice that if the exact figure is known (but cannot be explained in terms of a simple fraction), it must be added into the sentence. This is done in order to make the information more accurate, as well as more useful, for the reader. If the fraction is something like seven ninths, nine fourteenths or similar, do not use it because your aim is to summarise the data in an easy-to-read and fluent manner. For many people, fractions like these can be confusing. Look at the bar chart below and practice using the expressions shown above.

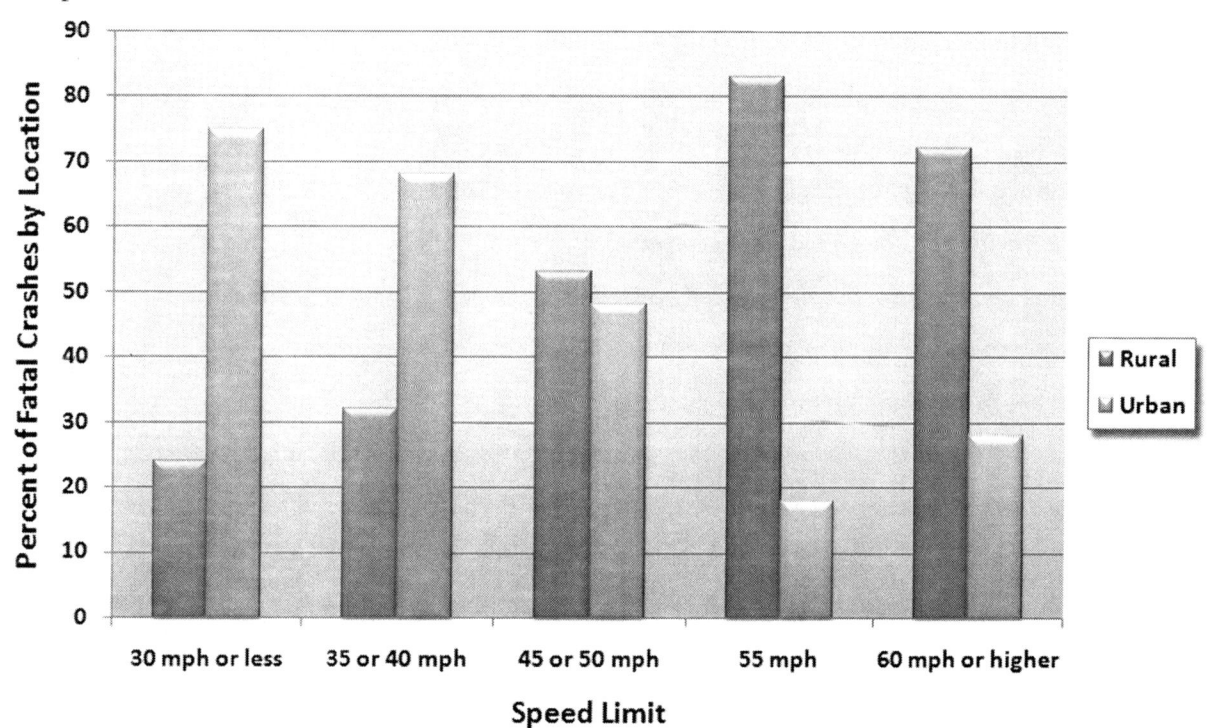

Surveys

Unit Five – Exercise D Page 126

Many diagrams are the result of a survey. They may be surveys that collect information by asking people about their opinion regarding various issues or statistical data about a whole range of topics, like illiteracy, Internet sales, pollution levels, GDP levels and so on. In the case of the latter. no people are actually questioned, but information is gathered from official data sources. Look at the table below and the results of a survey showing the reasons why men and women travelled overseas between 2006 and 2008. Decide if the sentences below are correct or incorrect. If the sentence is incorrect then decide how to alter it to make it correct.

Reasons	Percentage (%)
Holidays	87%
Business trips	63%
To study	9%
For a new job	12%
Medical reasons	26%
To do charity work	3%
Financial reasons	2%
To get married	9%
Visiting family or friends	35%
Conferences	16%

1. Just over a quarter of the people travelled abroad to visit their family or friends.
2. Slightly less than one in ten of those surveyed went abroad to study.
3. The same percentage of people travelled overseas to get a new job and to get married.
4. A little over a half of the people questioned travelled for business purposes.
5. Almost one in four moved for medical reasons.
6. Almost all of the people interviewed either went on business trips or visited family or friends.
7. Exactly a quarter of interviewees either studied or went to conferences.

Although you do not have to state the actual source of the survey, it can be useful to include a number of different phrases in your essay. For example, you could use phrases like the ones listed below.

1.	90% of the respondents stated that –
2.	The majority of both sexes were shown to have / be –
3.	37% of the women questioned felt that –
4.	Almost one third of women over 45 replied that –
5.	None of the respondents had / were –
6.	16% of the women surveyed had / were –
7.	The majority of the women in the survey –
8.	None of the respondents held the view that –
9.	The majority of both sexes who took part in the research said that –
10.	All age groups for both men and women considered _____ to be –

- **Copying Categories**

Many diagrams present categories which are only one word (possibly two) in length. However, whenever possible, try to use synonyms to replace the original wording.

Copying the names of cities or countries is not a problem, but from time to time you will see a diagram where each category could be three or more words in length. Unless these are terms or phrases which cannot, or should not, be changed, it is essential to alter them in some way.

Unit Five – Exercise E   Page 127

The results of this survey are shown as percentages. The sum of all of the percentages does not add up to 100%, so we know that many people chose more than one category as a reason for learning a foreign language.

Reasons for studying a foreign language	%
1. Study overseas	22%
2. Work overseas	7%
3. Business trips	36%
4. Husband / Wife is foreign	12%
5. Improve job prospects	18%
6. Make new friends	12%
7. Travel	54%
8. Company training policy	3%

A common mistake that students make is to copy the wording of each category. Doing this means they can end up writing sentences like,

The main business-related reason for studying a foreign language is Business trips at 36% which is exactly 50% less than Travel the largest personal reason (54%).

This is a problem for three reasons:

1.	The first is that unless the category is the title of, for example, a business or organization where the exact name needs to be written, copying is seen as a problem.
2.	The second is that phrases of three or more words in a diagram often need to be changed grammatically to fit into a complete sentence. Remember that the kind of grammar used for phrases in a diagram often misses out articles (**a, an, the**), prepositions (**in, on, at, for**) and so on. These need to be added when writing a complete sentence.
3.	Finally, capital letters should only be used if it is certain that the category is a title with the words remaining unchanged. The result is that many students not only copy too much from the diagram but also include grammar mistakes in many of their sentences.

If we take all of these points into consideration, we could change the original sentence into,

The main business-related reason for studying a foreign language was to use it on business trips at 36% which is exactly 50% less than those who wished to use it while travelling, the largest personal reason at 54%.

The key point here is to not be afraid to change phrases taken from the diagram. Doing this can only help increase your final grade. Also, notice that the categories have been divided into other groups – business-related reasons and personal reasons. We have seen before that this can help when writing general statements, but it has been used here as part of the main body.

Now try to write the 150-word essay. Think about using different synonyms to express the idea of a survey. Also, use the ideas of: business reasons and/or personal reasons for learning a language and their relative rankings, differences and similarities.

WRITING TASK 1

You should spend about 20 minutes on this task.

The diagram below shows information on Canada's 12 largest Aboriginal communities.

Summarise the information by selecting and reporting the main features, and make comparisons where relevant.

Write at least 150 words.

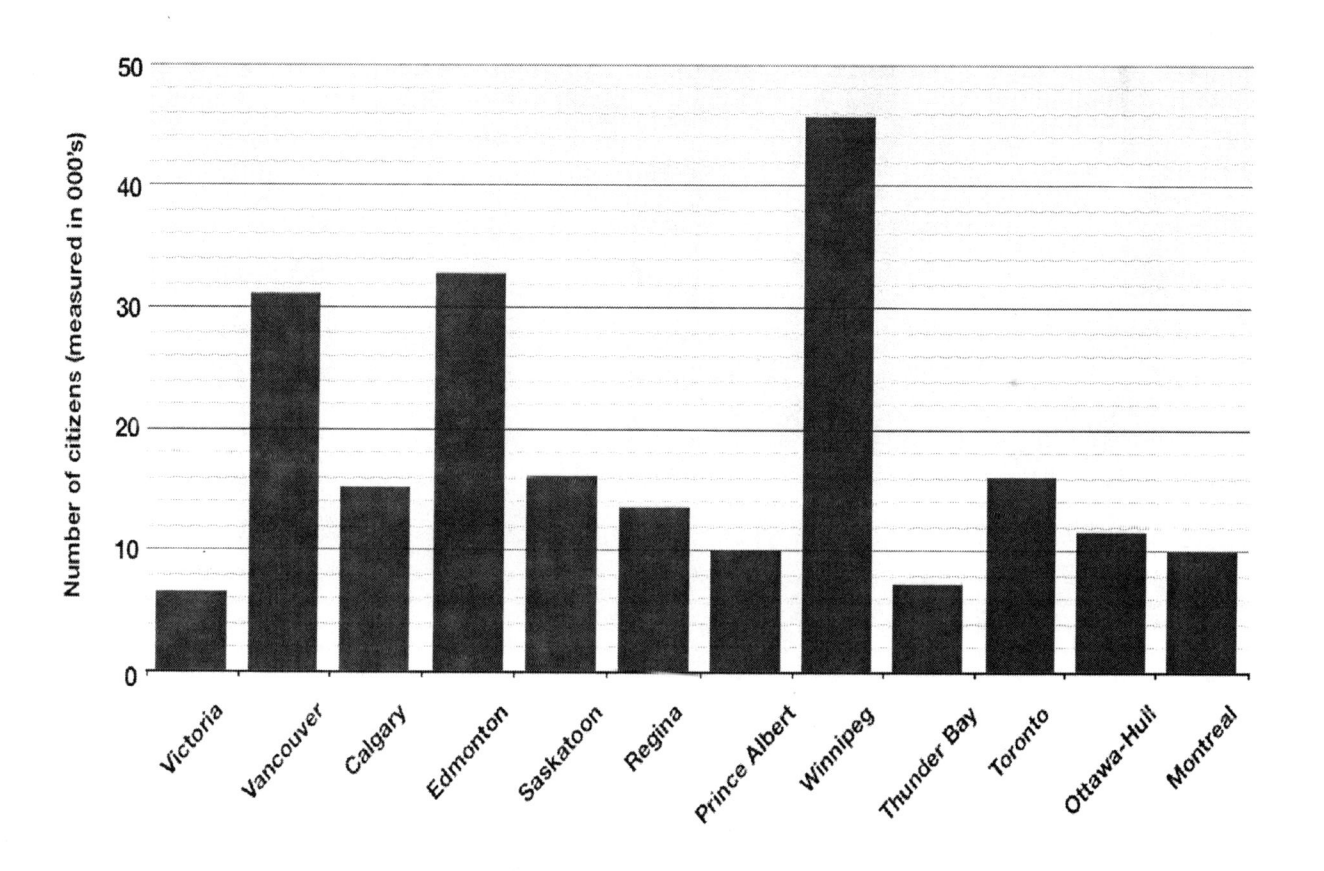

Canada's 12 largest urban aboriginal and metropolitan areas, 1996 census

City	Number of citizens (in 000's)
Victoria	~7
Vancouver	~31
Calgary	~15
Edmonton	~33
Saskatoon	~16
Regina	~13
Prince Albert	~10
Winnipeg	~45
Thunder Bay	~7
Toronto	~16
Ottawa-Hull	~11
Montreal	~10

Unit Five – Exercise G   Page 127

WRITING TASK 1

You should spend about 20 minutes on this task.

The diagram below shows information about carbon dioxide emissions for popular private jets.

Summarise the information by selecting and reporting the main features, and make comparisons where relevant.

Write at least 150 words.

Aircraft	Gallons/hr	Pounds (lbs.) of CO_2/hr	Flight cost/hr
Cessna CJ II	136	3,002	$2,700
Beechjet 400	182	4,017	$2,700
Hawker 400XP	188	4,149	$2,700
Cessna Citation XLS	204	4,502	$4,500
Learjet 60	209	4,613	$4,500
Hawker 800XP	188	4,149	$4,500
Gulfstream III	488	10,078	$6,750
Gulfstream 550	378	8,342	$6,750
Challenger 605	280	6,180	$6,750

Summary of Units Four and Five

Analysing Diagrams with a Time Period

YOU MUST

1.	turn every table into a line chart
2.	select some of the most important features of the diagram / the key points to look for are:

- the extremes - the constant - a peak - a trough	- only category to always rise / fall - biggest / smallest increase - two categories the same	- the continued rise / fall - comparison of change between two categories

3.	add words like – **predicted** – **expected** – **forecast** – **anticipated** – for the future
4.	use synonyms for **male** and **female**:

men women	girls boys	the opposite gender the opposite sex	their counterparts

	be careful when you are writing about younger people – children are not men and women
5.	use a variety of phrases when writing about activities:

boys like to participate in baseball girls like to take part in hockey	football is the favourite pastime pursuit meditation is the least favoured leisure time activity

6.	try to use different phrases when writing about age groups

YOU MUST NOT

1.	write about everything in the diagram
2.	use abbreviations for days and months
3.	use singular nouns if plural nouns are needed
4.	use opinions

Analysing Diagrams with no Time Period

	YOU MUST
1.	analyse the diagram by looking for:

- the extremes - two categories the same	- the relative size of one category with another - the rankings of one category to another

	- parts of a whole (only possible when working with percentages)
2.	use fractions as well as percentages whenever possible
3.	try to estimate figures, when they are not obvious, by using phrases like:

- just over / just under	- a little more / a little less than	- slightly over / slightly under

4.	Use different expressions when writing about a survey: - 90% of the respondents stated that - The majority of both sexes were shown to have / be - 37% of the women questioned felt that - Almost one third of women over 45 replied that - None of the respondents had / were - 16% of the women surveyed had / were - The majority of the women in the survey - None of the respondents held the view that - The majority of both sexes who took part in the research said that - All age groups for both men and women considered _____ to be
5.	correct the grammar of certain category titles, and paraphrase when necessary

	YOU MUST NOT
1.	use words or phrases that suggest there is a time period
2.	use the word **percentage** with figures. You can write **26 percent** but not **26 percentage**
3.	guess figures
4.	copy the name of each category unless it is impossible to paraphrase
5.	use opinions

UNIT SIX
Analysing Multiple Diagrams

The final part of learning how to write about bar charts, line charts, tables and pie charts is to look at Task 1 exercises with two or more diagrams in each example. You can have the same type of diagram in one exercise, or they might be different.

Writing about multiple diagrams is almost the same as for single diagrams. Therefore, you have already studied nearly everything you need to know. However, there are several more important points that need to be noted. Study Example A, and look at the introduction and general statement written below it.

Unit Six – Exercise A Page 128

Consumer preferences by media type

	Provides greatest experience	Is the most informative	Gives me the greatest pleasure	Is the first I turn on	Is the easiest to use
TV	46%	20%	22%	40%	42%
Magazines	3%	5%	3%	1%	3%
Newspapers	3%	23%	9%	12%	7%
Internet	27%	37%	49%	34%	24%
Radio	3%	4%	2%	9%	7%
All are equal	18%	11%	15%	5%	17%

Yesterday, did you...

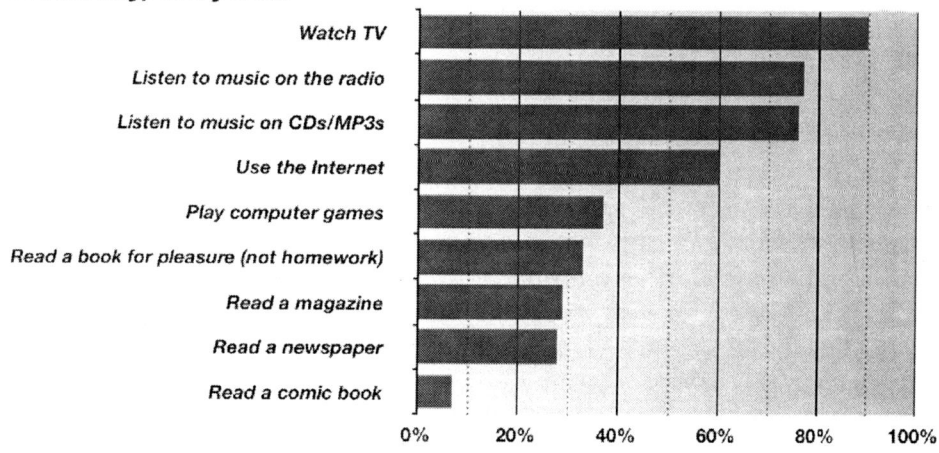

Activity	Percentage
Watch TV	~90%
Listen to music on the radio	~80%
Listen to music on CDs/MP3s	~75%
Use the Internet	~60%
Play computer games	~40%
Read a book for pleasure (not homework)	~35%
Read a magazine	~30%
Read a newspaper	~30%
Read a comic book	~5%

On a scale of one (very poor) to ten (very good), how good do you think the two paragraphs below are? Discuss your ideas with a classmate and decide what you like, dislike about them. If you think changes are needed you can rewrite them.

- **Introduction**

    The table compares and contrasts data on the preferences of people questioned for five different types of media. The bar chart compares and contrasts data on the nine activities favoured by 13 to 17 year olds.

- **General Statement**

    In general, the TV was voted as providing the greatest experience while the Internet was the most informative and gave people the greatest sense of control, and finally the TV was what people turned on first and was the easiest to use. The majority of the 13 to 17 year olds watched TV and the minority of them read a comic book.

The main problem here is that the two paragraphs add up to 98 words, so this is far more than the recommended 50 to 60 words. The main reasons for this are that,

- two sentences have been used for each paragraph
- too much information has been added
- some repetition of information has also occurred

The way to avoid this is to use only one sentence for each paragraph and think about using a phrase like, **The two diagrams compare and contrast** for the introduction and, **An overview of the diagrams shows that** for the general statement to start each paragraph.

Writing such long paragraphs tells the examiner that you are not able to select the most important points for each paragraph. Your ability to write in a concise manner suffers as a result. Do be careful, sometimes Task 1 statements are written longer than they should be. This is done to see if you follow the same style. If you do, you will end up with an even longer paragraph but probably a lower grade. Now try to write the whole essay.

- **Main Body**

Although many students think multiple diagrams are more difficult, it is fairly easy to see why this is not true. So far, all of the diagrams in this book have been single diagrams, and you have had to write about 100 words for each main body. With a multiple diagram you have the same number of words to write but you can use data from two or more diagrams. This means that each diagram provides some of the data you need and so offers more information to choose from. Also, you can still look for the same key points that you looked for with single diagrams, with and without time periods. The final point is that you need to decide whether or not it is possible to compare and contrast between each diagram. When do you think it could be possible? Why might it not be possible?

Unit Six – Exercise B   Page 128

WRITING TASK 1

You should spend about 20 minutes on this task.

The diagrams below show the results of a survey from Taiwan explaining how students, wanting to study overseas, chose a university from 1998 – 2008.

Summarise the information by selecting and reporting the main features, and make comparisons where relevant.

Write at least 150 words.

MALE

	1998	2008
Ranking	97%	95%
Cost of tuition	88%	97%
Location	18%	32%
Modern teaching facilities	66%	42%
Good language support	73%	61%
Quality of teachers	13%	6%
Cost of accommodation	92%	86%
Modern teaching methods	8%	7%

FEMALE

	1998	2008
Ranking	100%	90%
Cost of tuition	93%	95%
Location	11%	25%
Modern teaching facilities	72%	76%
Good language support	39%	21%
Quality of teachers	5%	7%
Cost of accommodation	91%	93%
Modern teaching methods	5%	2%

Unit Six – Exercise C

Page 128

WRITING TASK 1

You should spend about 20 minutes on this task.

The charts below show the amount of area used for growing fruit between 1993 and 2006 in Washington State (USA).

Summarise the information by selecting and reporting the main features, and make comparisons where relevant.

Write at least 150 words.

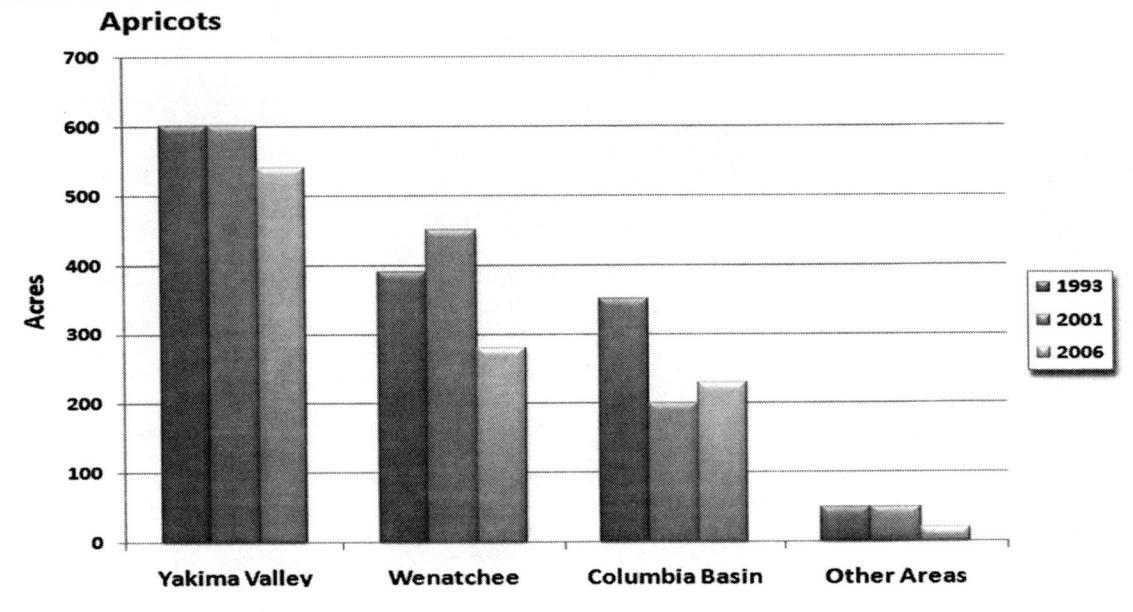

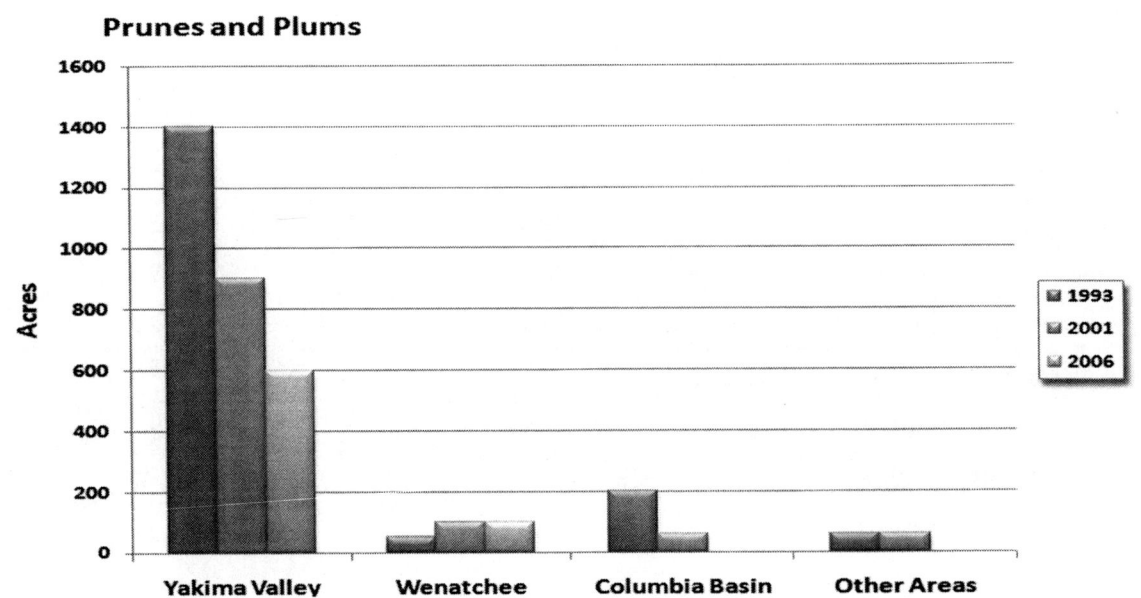

Apricots

Prunes and Plums

Unit Six – Exercise D

WRITING TASK 1

You should spend about 20 minutes on this task.

The charts below show the consumption of various food groups by people in the UK, 1942 – 2004/5.

Summarise the information by selecting and reporting the main features, and make comparisons where relevant.

Write at least 150 words.

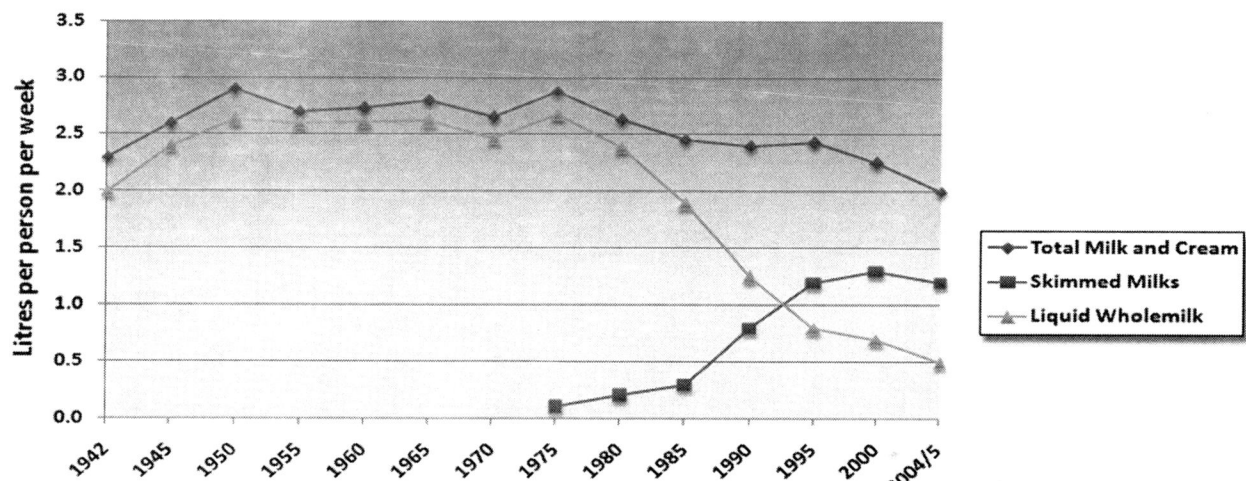

Consumption of Milk and Milk Products

(Litres per person per week; 1942–2004/5)
- Total Milk and Cream
- Skimmed Milks
- Liquid Wholemilk

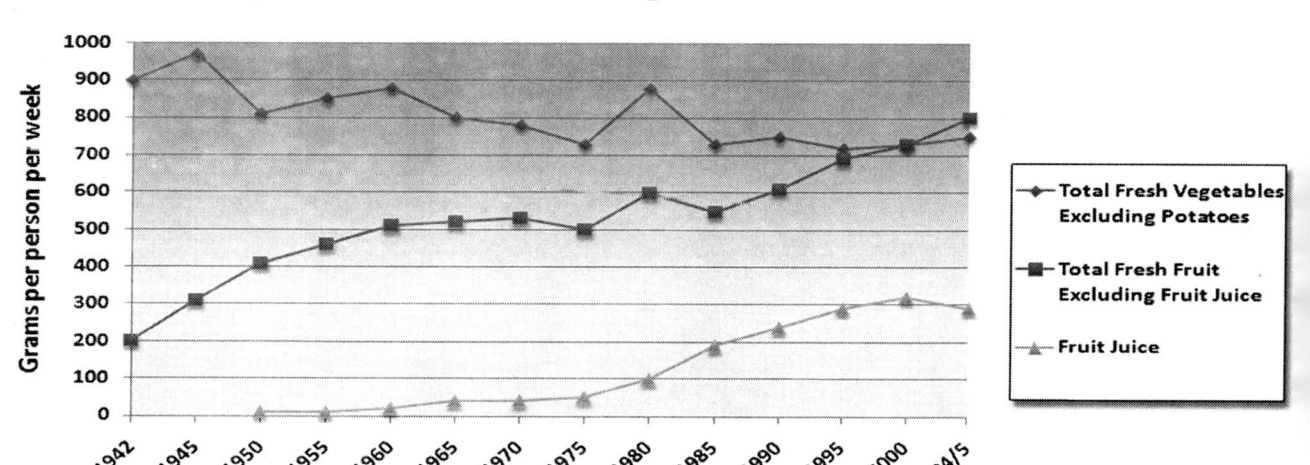

Consumption of Fresh Fruit and Vegetables

(Grams per person per week; 1942–2004/5)
- Total Fresh Vegetables Excluding Potatoes
- Total Fresh Fruit Excluding Fruit Juice
- Fruit Juice

Unit Six – Exercise E

WRITING TASK 1

You should spend about 20 minutes on this task.

The charts below show information about the top five supermarkets in the UK.

Summarise the information by selecting and reporting the main features, and make comparisons where relevant.

Write at least 150 words.

Supermarkets- how the big five compare

Number of UK Stores

- Tesco — Employees in UK: 200,000 — 119
- Asda — Employees in UK: 117,000 — 480
- J. Sainsbury — Employees in UK: 174,000 — 463
- Safeway — Employees in UK: 92,000 — 258
- Morrisons — Employees in UK: 46,000 — 730

UK Market Share, September 2003

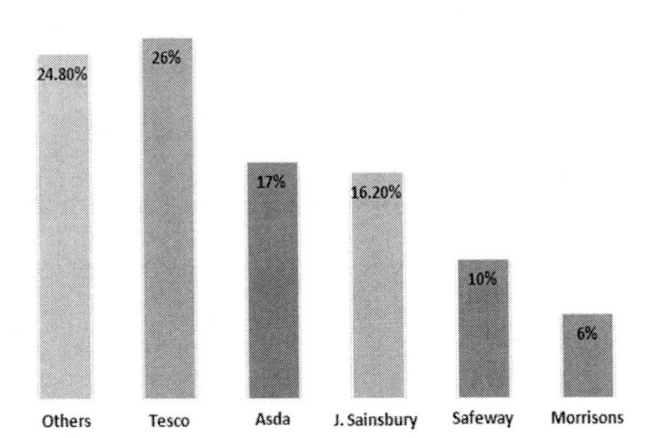

Others	Tesco	Asda	J. Sainsbury	Safeway	Morrisons
24.80%	26%	17%	16.20%	10%	6%

Summary of Unit Six

Analysing Multiple Diagrams

Writing about multiple diagrams is almost the same as for single diagrams. Therefore, you have already studied nearly everything you need to know in the previous units. You can review the summaries for the previous units if you need to refresh your memory.

However, there are several more important points that need to be noted, so look at the key points listed below.

YOU MUST	
1.	use one paragraph for the introduction
2.	use one paragraph for the general statement
3.	compare and contrast between each diagram if it is possible to do so. As a general rule, if the two diagrams are of the same type (e.g. two bar charts) there is a much greater chance that it is possible to compare and contrast between them. Also, if the two charts could be combined into one (e.g. If one diagram is about men, the other about women) they can probably be compared and contrasted.

YOU MUST NOT	
1.	use two or more sentences for the introduction
2.	use two or more sentences for the general statement
3.	add too much information in either the introduction or general statement
4.	repeat information
5.	use opinions

Getting Started – Again!

Many IELTS students, when they take the test, are lucky and are given a bar chart, line chart, pie chart or table to write about. If they have prepared well, by studying hard and practising a lot, they should get good results. You could, however, find something completely different on the test paper in front of you. It might be,

1	a process	- that shows how something is manufactured
2	a cycle	- like the water cycle or carbon dioxide cycle
3	a flow chart	- similar to a process but often used to explain how decisions are made or what actions are taken
4	an object	- like the Eiffel Tower whose features you have to describe - like an air conditioner whose function must be described
5	a map	- showing changes that have occurred over a period of time - with several possible construction sites for something like a new building (supermarket, school), motorway or airport and you must write about the advantages and disadvantages of each

If this comes as a shock to you, then the rest of this book has been written for you in mind. These other Task 1 diagrams are completely different from those written about in the first part of this book. In fact many students, particularly those that try to self-study, don't know about these other types of diagram because it can be very difficult to find information about them. Other students simply think they won't be in the test. This book has also been written with these people in mind and the need to tell you, **YES – these diagrams can be in your test**.

It is absolutely essential that you spend time – much more time than most students do – in studying these diagrams. Taking the test when you are unprepared, can mean that you have a much greater chance of getting a low IELTS grade. This can be avoided with a little time and patience.

Although many of the diagrams listed above seem quite different from one another, they do have one main feature in common. Regardless of which type of diagram you have to write about, they all need to be very descriptive in form. In other words, you have to describe the information contained in the diagram in a very clear, concise way. Also, all Task 1 essays need to be at least 150 words, and this remains true for these other types of diagram. Again, apart from one type of Task 1 diagram that you will read about later, you cannot use opinions as a way to make your essay longer. As you work through the rest of this book and do the various exercises provided, you will develop the skills, and the confidence you need to write a good Task 1 essay.

UNIT SEVEN

Processes

● Definition

A process can be thought of as a series of actions or changes that happen in a set order to produce a desired result. Or, put more simply, a process shows you how something is <u>made or changed in some</u> way.

● Introduction

Spend a little time looking at the diagram below, and think about how you would write an introduction. You can see that writing an introduction for a process is going to be very different from a regular Task 1 introduction. You do not need, for instance, to compare and contrast anything, there is no time period, no units to consider and no groups or categories to list.

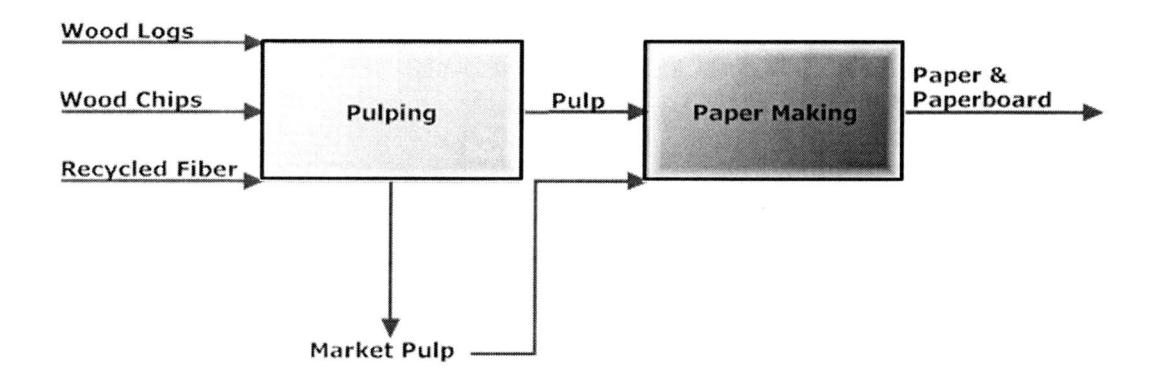

All you need to do is explain very clearly what kind of process this is. In this case, how paper and paper board are made. You could, therefore, write something like,

> *The illustration presented highlights the various stages involved in the production of paper and paperboard from three <u>original ingredients</u>.*

or

> *The diagram details the different steps needed to produce paper and paperboard from three original ingredients.*

71

Unit Seven – Exercise A

To see how easy writing an introduction for a process is, write introductions for the following,

1. the production of essential oils
2. the purification of water

Even if you do not know what **essential oils** are, it is still possible to write an introduction stating that this is a process about their production. Equally, if you do not know what **purification** is, you can still write a good introduction stating that this is a purification process.

- **General Statement**

With a partner, try to decide what kind of general statement you would write for the diagram showing the paper making process on the previous page. What kind of information would act as an overview of this process?

- **Main Body**

As you have probably already realized, you do not need to write a general statement. You simply move from the introduction to the main body. With no general statement to write the main body needs to be about 130 words in length.

- **Conclusion**

If you develop the diagram fully, writing an introduction and a main body will be enough. However, if you finish the process and the total number of words written is less than 150 you have a problem.

It would probably be very difficult, in a situation like this, to go back over your essay and add extra information. The solution, therefore, is to simply add a conclusion. These are not actually required but can be added if needed. A typical conclusion for the production of chocolate would look like this,

All of the stages involved in the production of chocolate have now been completed and chocolate has been produced from the original ingredients of cocoa beans, milk and sugar.

Note the use of the present perfect passive verb form – **has been produced**.

Using the correct writing style

Like all forms of writing, you must also decide on the correct writing style. Look at part of a recipe explaining the process for making chocolate sponge cake.

Place the baking trays in the centre of the pre-heated oven and cook for 30 minutes. You must not open the oven door during this time. After 30 minutes you can take the trays out of the oven and leave them for one minute to slightly cool. Turn the trays upside down onto a wire rack and remove the cakes. You must let them cool completely before removing the grease proof paper.

Do you think this is informal or formal? Discuss with your classmate whether or not it is the correct style to use and, if not, what could be done to improve it.

The key point to remember is, when writing about any process in IELTS Task 1 writing, you must NOT have any direct or indirect reference to people. This means that you cannot use words like – **you, they, we, people, I** – in your essay. These are direct references to people and are used more often in an informal style of writing. Academic writing, however, is seen as being more formal and usually has no (or very few) direct references to people.

Taking out any reference to people makes it a typical style for writing recipes but still the wrong style for academic purposes. This is because sentences like - **Place the baking trays in the centre of the pre-heated oven and cook for 30 minutes** - tell someone how to do something and is still an indirect reference to people.

This means that the style of writing is not formal enough. So the question is, therefore, how do you change a sentence that has an indirect reference into a more formal style? To do this you must use the passive form of the verb.

Look at the example.

Place the baking trays in the centre of the pre-heated oven and cook for 30 minutes.

The verbs can be turned from the simple present (**Active**) into the simple present (**Passive**).

The baking trays are placed in the centre of the pre-heated oven and are then cooked for 30 minutes.

One problem, however, is trying to decide if a verb is regular or irregular. In this example it is regular and follows the rule: **is / are <u>verb + ed</u> (regular)**. Unfortunately, if you do not know for sure if the verb is regular or irregular the only thing you can do is guess.

Understanding the Diagram

There are several important features that are always important to look for in the diagram. They help you understand the process more fully. In the paper making process diagram, you can see that there are a lot of arrows moving in either a horizontal or vertical direction.

Horizontal arrow ⟶   **Vertical arrow** ↑

These are typical of a process and represent the direction of movement from one stage to the next, and the various changes that occur in it. They also help you to decide which part of the process is the beginning. The examiner would not be impressed if you picked the wrong part of the process to start your essay.

In other processes, you might see that numbers are used either with, or without, arrows. In this case, simply describe what happens starting with number one, and move through the various stages in order. If a diagram has neither arrows nor numbers then logic (western style) tells us that the flow of events is probably in a left to right direction. The paper making process, however, seems to have three different starting points. They all go in the same direction, and all of them go to the next stage in this process, so you can combine them into one sentence.

Another very important part of understanding the diagram, is to read every word that is in it. This helps to explain the relationship between each stage and the kind of changes that are taking place. By understanding the process more clearly, you will find it much easier to write a main body in a concise but clear manner.

However, if you think about how many millions of products are produced around the world, that gives you some idea of how many different process diagrams are possible. This means the chances of having a process that contains words you don't understand are quite high. Nevertheless, you are still expected to be able to develop the information enough to complete the essay.

Verb Selection

While looking at the diagram, it is also a good idea to start thinking about which verbs you might use when writing the main body. Processes are not like the more typical Task 1 diagrams where you know that you can always use verbs like increase, decrease or their synonyms. Here, the verbs you select will vary from diagram to diagram, so you need to be more careful in selecting the verbs you need. Using verbs that do not describe accurately what is happening will help lower your grade.

Look at the two processes below (Examples B and C) and decide which verbs you might use to write the main body. Try to find some verbs in the information already provided in each diagram, and think of others that might be needed.

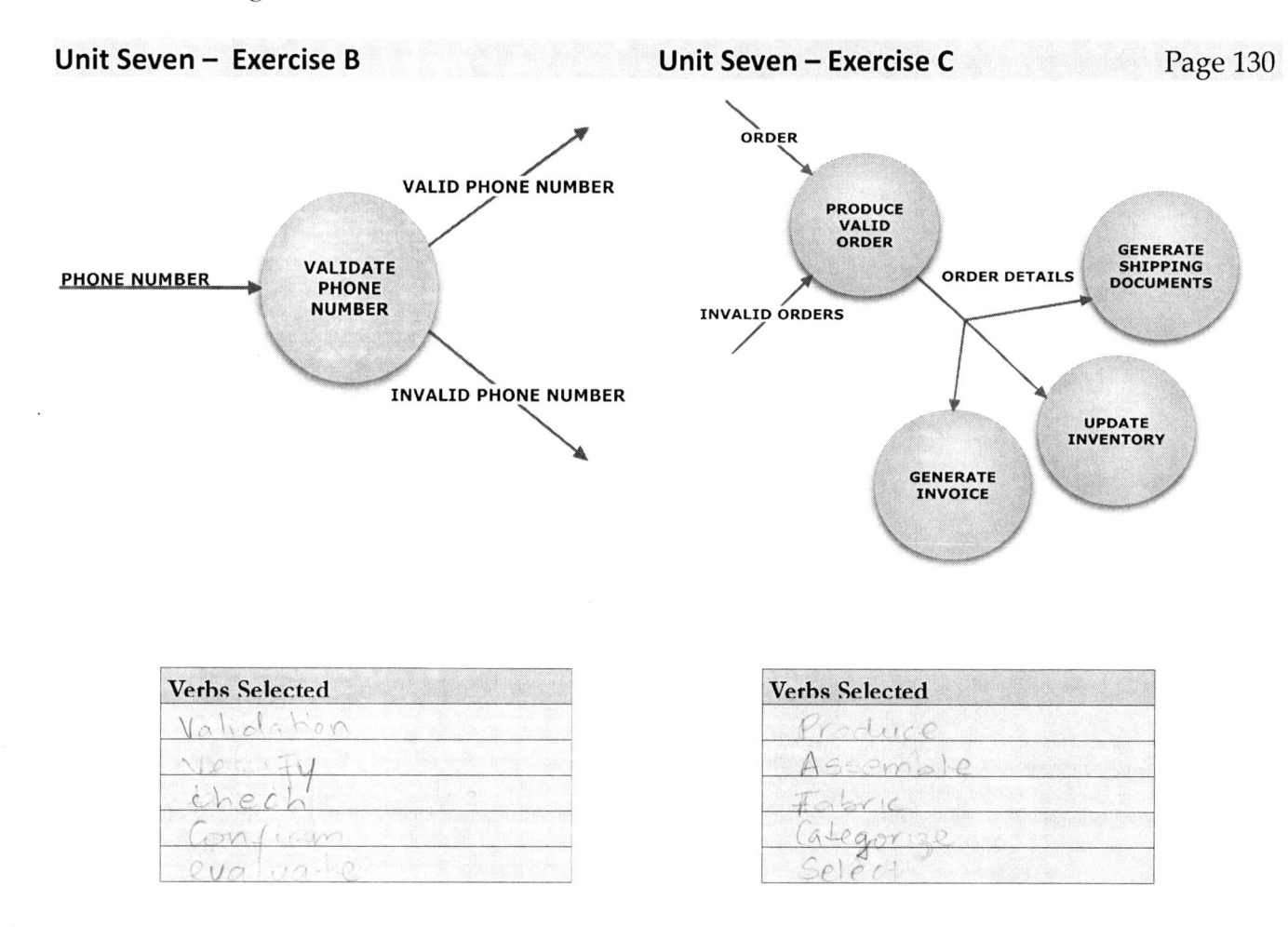

Unit Seven – Exercise B

PHONE NUMBER → VALIDATE PHONE NUMBER → VALID PHONE NUMBER / INVALID PHONE NUMBER

Verbs Selected
- Validation
- Verify
- check
- Confirm
- evaluate

Unit Seven – Exercise C

Page 130

ORDER → PRODUCE VALID ORDER → ORDER DETAILS → GENERATE SHIPPING DOCUMENTS / UPDATE INVENTORY / GENERATE INVOICE / INVALID ORDERS

Verbs Selected
- Produce
- Assemble
- Fabric
- Categorize
- Select

Selecting the correct Verb Tense

For all processes, with a few exceptions, you use the **simple present tense** when writing about processes. This verb tense is preferred, not because a process is a fact, (something many students suggest as a reason to use the simple present) but because it is a routine or habit and, therefore, something that happens regularly. In the same way, if the examiner asks you to talk about a typical weekend or day at work, you would also use the simple present tense because you are talking about your routine or habit.

Look at Examples B and C again, and write a few sentences describing what happens in each process. Use the verbs that you selected. Try to keep the sentences simple, but concise, and make sure that you write about each stage in order. When you have finished, discuss your sentences with a classmate.

Unit Seven – Exercise D Page 130

Now look at the beer making process below, and complete the essay by adding the correct verb form from the verbs in brackets.

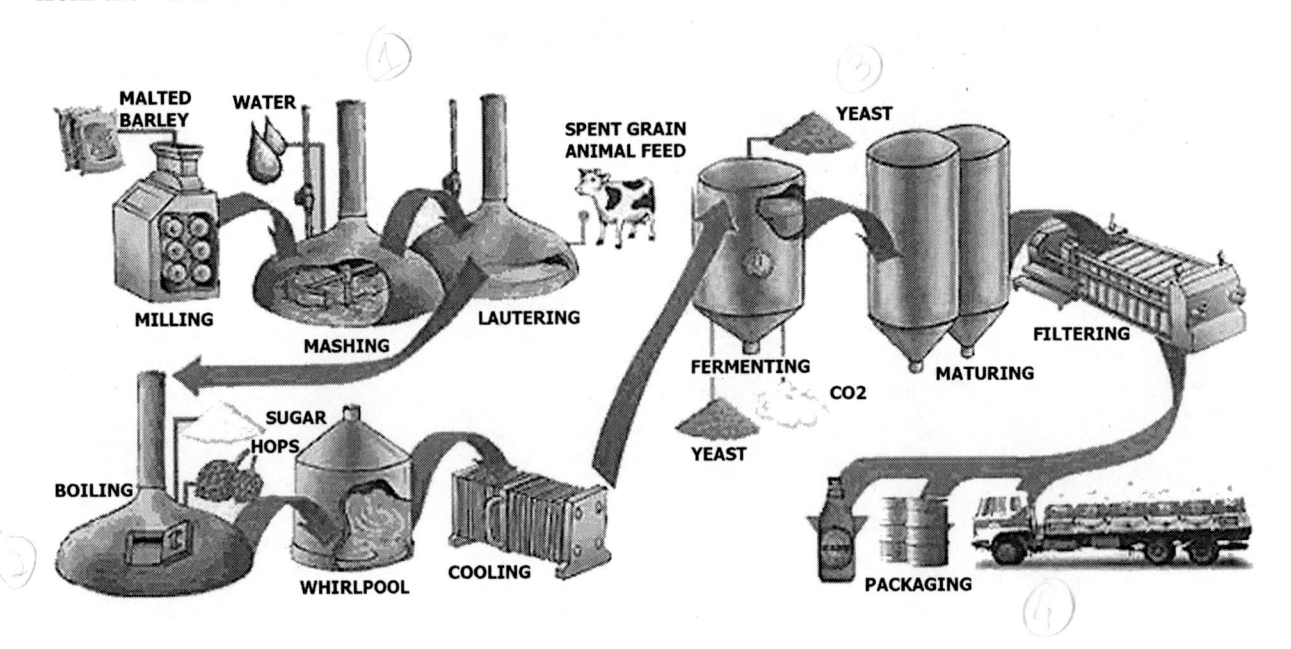

The illustration .... (present) highlights the various stages involved (involve) in the production of beer from the original ingredients of malted barley, hops, sugar, yeast and water.

The whole beer production process .... (start) when malted barley .... (mill) before .... (add) to water and then .... (mash). Following the mashing process it .... (enter) the lautering phase which results in malted barley that is then .... (boil) along with hops and sugar. Spent grain is also produced as a by-product which .... (feed) to cattle as feed. Once .... (boil) the material enters a whirlpool and is subsequently cooled before entering a large fermentation tank. It is at this stage that yeast .... (add) to the mix. During this particular stage carbon dioxide is produced and once fermentation is complete the yeast is also discarded. The liquid then .... (enter) a maturation phase before .... (filter) and then bottled, canned or .... (put) into tankers for transportation.

76

Unit Seven – Exercise E   Page 131

Use the verbs from the box below, and complete the essay by putting the verbs into the correct form. Not all of the verbs need to be used.

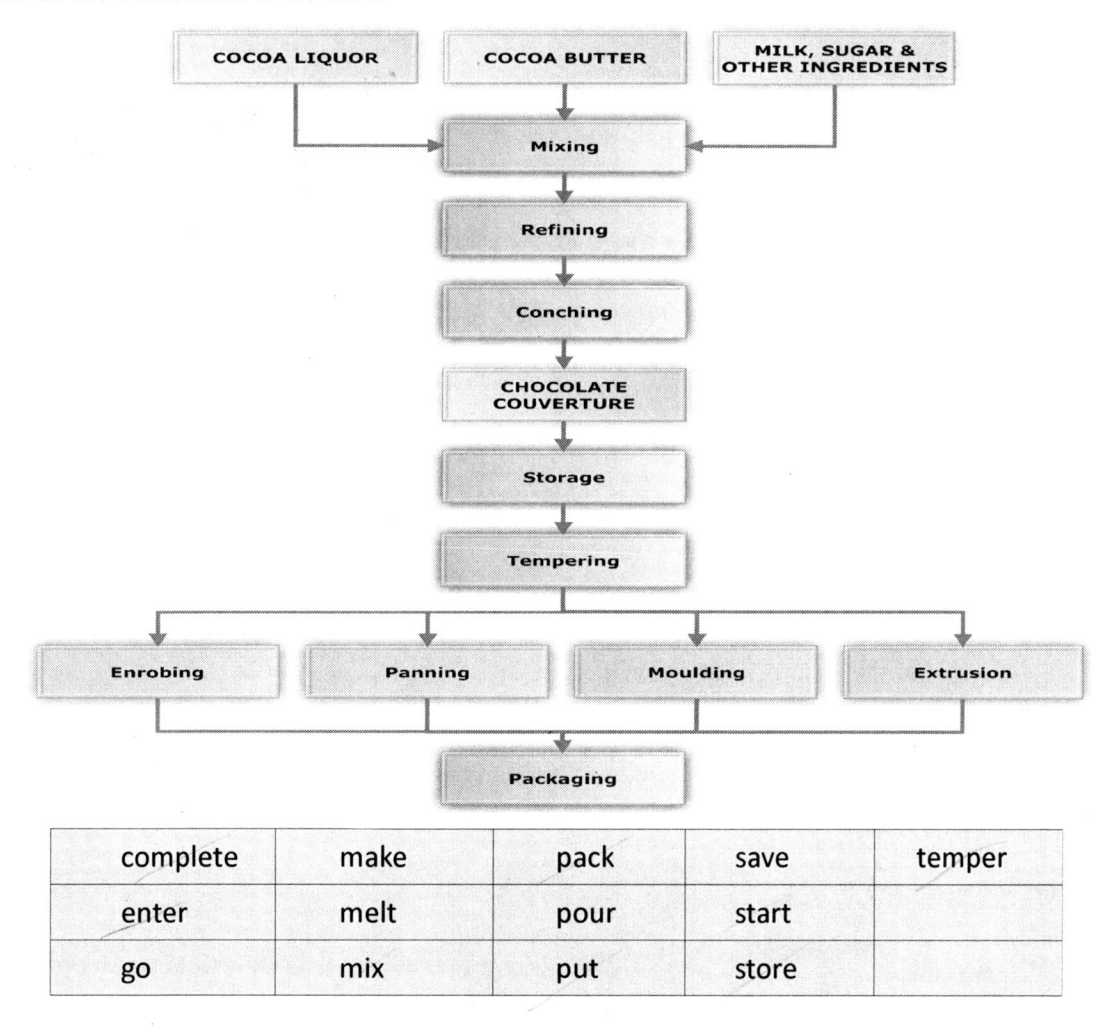

```
        COCOA LIQUOR      COCOA BUTTER      MILK, SUGAR & OTHER INGREDIENTS
                    │           │              │
                    └──────► Mixing ◄──────────┘
                              │
                           Refining
                              │
                           Conching
                              │
                       CHOCOLATE COUVERTURE
                              │
                           Storage
                              │
                          Tempering
                  ┌───────────┼───────────┬───────────┐
              Enrobing     Panning     Moulding    Extrusion
                  └───────────┴─────┬─────┴───────────┘
                                Packaging
```

complete	make	pack	save	temper
enter	melt	pour	start	
go	mix	put	store	

The illustration presented highlights the main stages involved in the production of chocolate from four main ingredients.

The manufacturing of chocolate ………….. with the ………….. of cocoa liquor, cocoa butter, milk, sugar and a range of other ingredients. After these have been thoroughly blended together the mixture ………….. the refining stage of production. Once this particular stage in the manufacturing process ………….., it is then followed by conching a process that results in a mixture called the chocolate couverture. The couverture ………….. for a period of time before it ………….. Subsequently, four different and penultimate processes are carried out simultaneously. These are enrobing, panning, moulding and extrusion which then lead to the final stage of this process where the chocolate ………….. into packaging.

All of the stages involved in making chocolate have now been completed and chocolate …………..

Example D and E are good examples of how to write a process in a formal style. However, do note that it was not always necessary to use the passive voice. Other verb forms were also used.

- **Developing each stage more fully**

As explained earlier, if each stage in this process is not developed fully, it becomes more and more difficult to write 150 words. Writing a conclusion still might not add enough words to the essay. To help with this, it is very important to make sure that a number of different requirements are fulfilled. The first is that each piece of information flows smoothly into the next. Words, known as time order phrases, help link each part of the process together. As you begin to practice writing processes, try to use a different time order phrase each time you move from one stage to the next. You will find that these are also used when writing cycles and flow charts.

Time Order Phrases		
Next	After this	Secondly
Then	Initially	Finally
Subsequently	At first	Following this
Once this particular stage in the process has been completed		
When this has been done		

Also, writing more fully about each stage is an important key to writing 150 words. If we take Example F, showing the steam distillation process used in the manufacture of eucalyptus essential oil, you can see that there are several ways you can write about each stage.

Unit Seven – Exercise F   Page 131

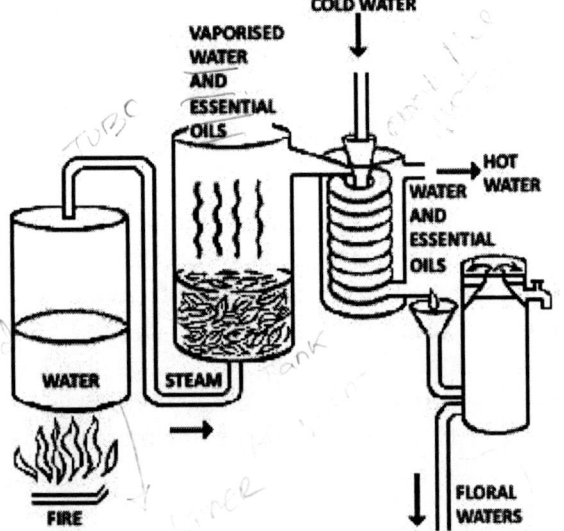

One way to write a main body would be to only use the information from the diagram. For example,

The first stage is fire and water. After this there is steam and then vaporized water and essential oils. Cold water goes in and after this water and essential oils become the hot water, essential oils and floral waters.

There are obviously many problems with this,

1. The main body is far too short and only uses information taken from the diagram.
2. Verb selection is very limited.
3. Each stage in the process has not been developed clearly and concisely.
4. Sentence structures are simple and badly written.
5. The phrase, *vaporized water and essential oils*, has been copied directly from the diagram.
6. It is very obvious that the writer does not understand the process.

It is essential to try and understand the process as much as possible because you can then add implied information about each stage. For example, a different approach in writing this essay would be to write phrases like: …… **water is heated in an enclosed container** …… and …… **the steam produced by this action enters a tube** ……

Spend a few minutes studying the diagram again, and write the whole essay by developing each stage as much as possible.

Developing your vocabulary

A big part of not being able to develop a process enough is often caused by a limited vocabulary range. As mentioned earlier, you might find that some of the words in a diagram are difficult to understand. This is often because you might not be so familiar with the particular process being described. If this happens, try to use the illustrations to help you follow the process more easily, and highlight the words that you know. As you look at some of the examples shown in this unit, you will probably find that you have to write about subjects that you have no knowledge about. How many of you, for example, know how to make paper, biofuel, Pu'er tea, sake and so on and so on? Regardless of the process being described, you are still expected to be able to write an essay explaining all of the stages shown.

If you do have a process in your test, and have experience about what is shown, you are very lucky. Understanding what is happening in the process makes it much easier to develop the main body. Knowing even a little about what you are writing about will give you more confidence, and enable you to focus more clearly on writing a good essay.

A more likely scenario, however, is that you will have to write about a process that you have never thought about. Also, words will be used that you have never seen before. It is at this stage that many IELTS students suddenly feel the need to improve their vocabulary range. Of course, this is an excellent idea and can be done over a period of time by reading newspapers, magazines, novels. Indeed reading anything in English is useful. Do not think that every word you learn has to come from an English textbook. The more English you are exposed to, the quicker you will increase your vocabulary.

The problem, however, is that most students do not have much time to learn new words before their test. A need to meet a deadline – the test – often means that there is a race against time to learn all of the skills needed to ensure a high grade. Trying to find time to learn more words becomes extremely difficult. Another problem is that you don't know which words you will need in the test. You might be increasing your vocabulary by using some of the ideas suggested above but, until your vocabulary range becomes very extensive, you are unlikely to be learning enough of the words used in these diagrams.

IELTS examiners, when deciding what grade to give to you, will take vocabulary selection into account. Typically, specific nouns and verbs will be given to you in the diagram but, despite this kind of help, many verbs still need to be chosen by you and will often contribute more than nouns to your final grade. Of course, if some verbs are already in the diagram, try to use synonyms whenever possible.

More advanced students might find it possible to take verbs used in the diagram, and change them into other forms of the same word. For example, **production** can become **produce**, **fertilisation** can become **fertilise, deliver** becomes **delivery** and so on.

This skill takes time, and a fairly extensive vocabulary range, but it is important to work on improving this skill.

● Purpose for Doing Something

Another useful way of developing the main body is by including information that explains why a certain action is done. Look at the list below showing a range of different phrases that can be used.

1	After this the leaves are left outside in the sun <u>in order that</u> they can be sun-dried.
2	After this they are left outside <u>as this</u> allows them to sun dry.
3	Following the mashing process it enters the lautering phase <u>which results in</u> malted barley
4	As they do so, cold water is passed through the middle of the coil <u>because this</u> allows the water to condense and some of it then leaves as hot water through a pipe.
5	After this particular stage has finished, the sake is filtered <u>so that</u> any impurities can be removed.
6	This mixture then undergoes a process called dilute acid esterification <u>which enables</u> these products to be transformed chemically.
7	The wind blows the vapour to a higher altitude <u>which allows</u> them to cool and form rain clouds.
8	The shipping documents need to be prepared, the invoice itself and finally the inventory is updated <u>to ensure that</u> sufficient stock is available.

Unit Seven – Exercise G   Page 131

Look at the example below of part of a process to manufacture cheese. Try to change the words in the table into other forms of the same word. More than one answer may be possible.

Part of the Cheese Manufacturing Processing

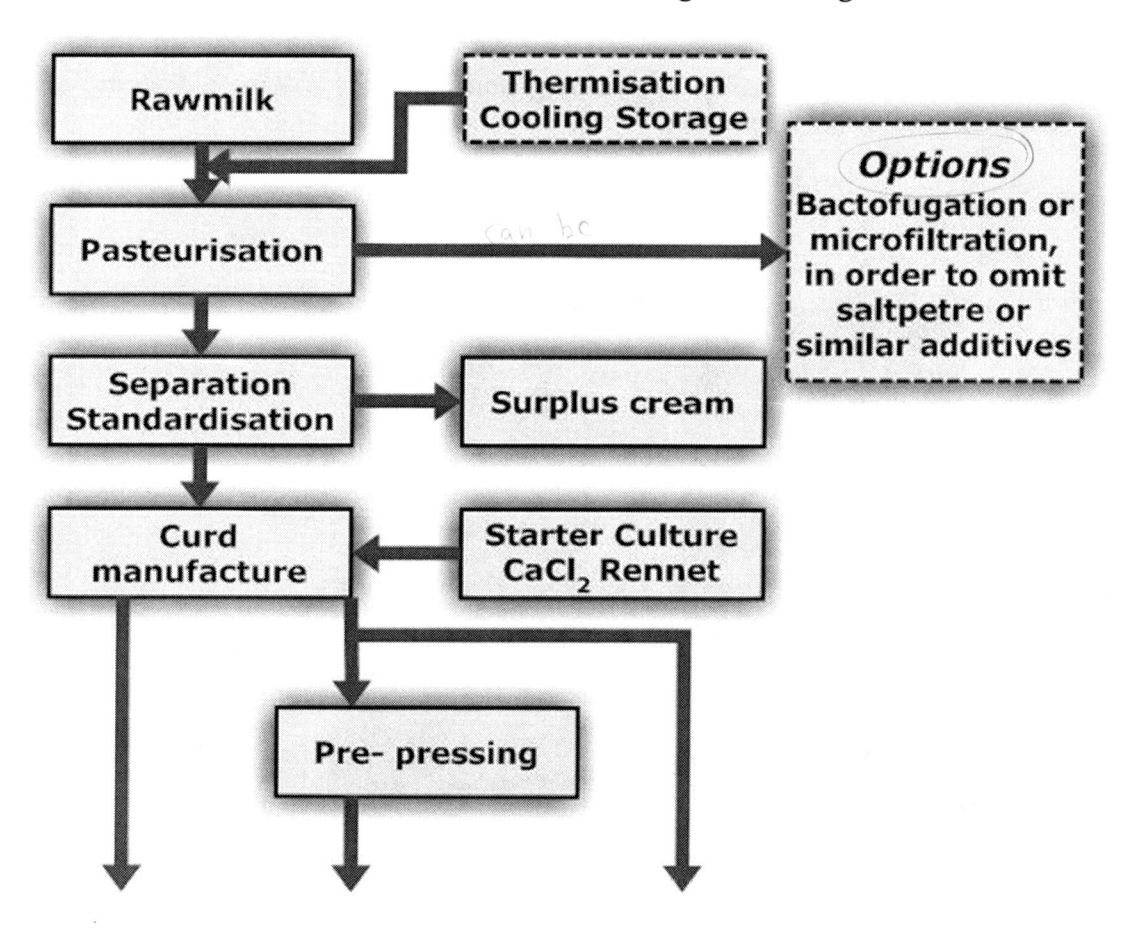

Rawmilk → Pasteurisation
Thermisation Cooling Storage → Rawmilk
Pasteurisation *can be* → Options: Bactofugation or microfiltration, in order to omit saltpetre or similar additives
Pasteurisation → Separation Standardisation → Surplus cream
Separation Standardisation → Curd manufacture
Starter Culture CaCl$_2$ Rennet → Curd manufacture
Curd manufacture → Pre- pressing

Original Word	New Word	Original Word	New Word
thermisation	*(increasing temperature)*	starter	beginners
cooling	*decrease temp*	pre-pressing	
pasteurisation		bactofugation	
separation	divide	microfiltration	filtrate
standardisation		omit	

81

Unit Seven – Exercise H

WRITING TASK 1

You should spend about 20 minutes on this task.

> *The diagram below shows information about the production of Pu'er tea.*
>
> *Summarise the information by selecting and reporting the main features, and make comparisons where relevant.*

Write at least 150 words.

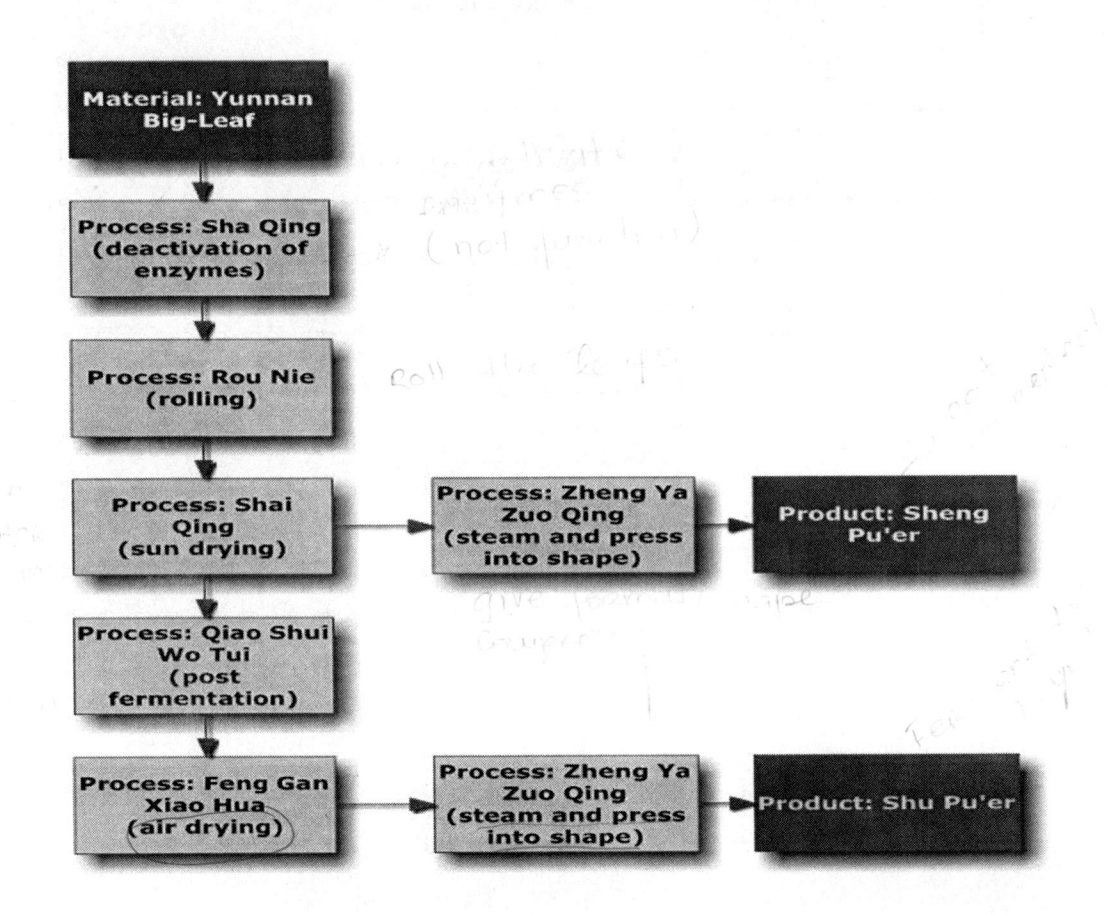

Flow diagram:

- Material: Yunnan Big-Leaf
  - ↓
- Process: Sha Qing (deactivation of enzymes)
  - ↓
- Process: Rou Nie (rolling)
  - ↓
- Process: Shai Qing (sun drying)
  - → Process: Zheng Ya Zuo Qing (steam and press into shape) → Product: Sheng Pu'er
  - ↓
- Process: Qiao Shui Wo Tui (post fermentation)
  - ↓
- Process: Feng Gan Xiao Hua (air drying)
  - → Process: Zheng Ya Zuo Qing (steam and press into shape) → Product: Shu Pu'er

Unit Seven – Exercise I   Page 132

WRITING TASK 1

You should spend about 20 minutes on this task.

The diagram below shows information about the production of sake.

Summarise the information by selecting and reporting the main features, and make comparisons where relevant.

Write at least 150 words.

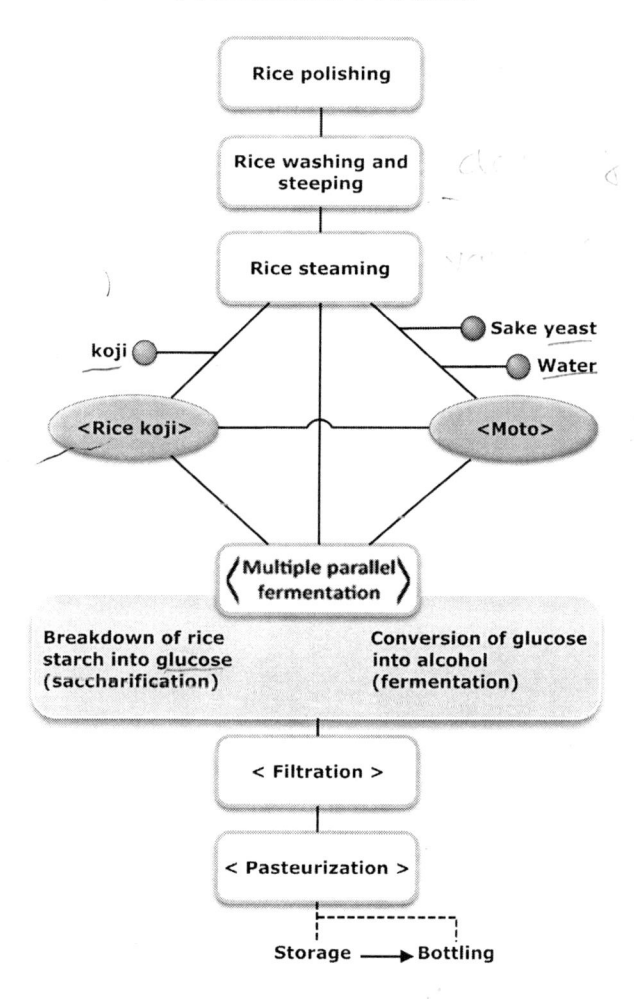

An Overview of the Sake Production Process

Rice polishing
↓
Rice washing and steeping
↓
Rice steaming

koji ● ──── <Rice koji>
Sake yeast ●
Water ●
<Moto>

↓
Multiple parallel fermentation

Breakdown of rice starch into glucose (saccharification)
Conversion of glucose into alcohol (fermentation)

↓
< Filtration >
↓
< Pasteurization >
↓
Storage ⟶ Bottling

Unit Seven – Exercise J

WRITING TASK 1

You should spend about 20 minutes on this task.

The diagram below shows information about the production of biofuels.

Summarise the information by selecting and reporting the main features, and make comparisons where relevant.

Write at least 150 words.

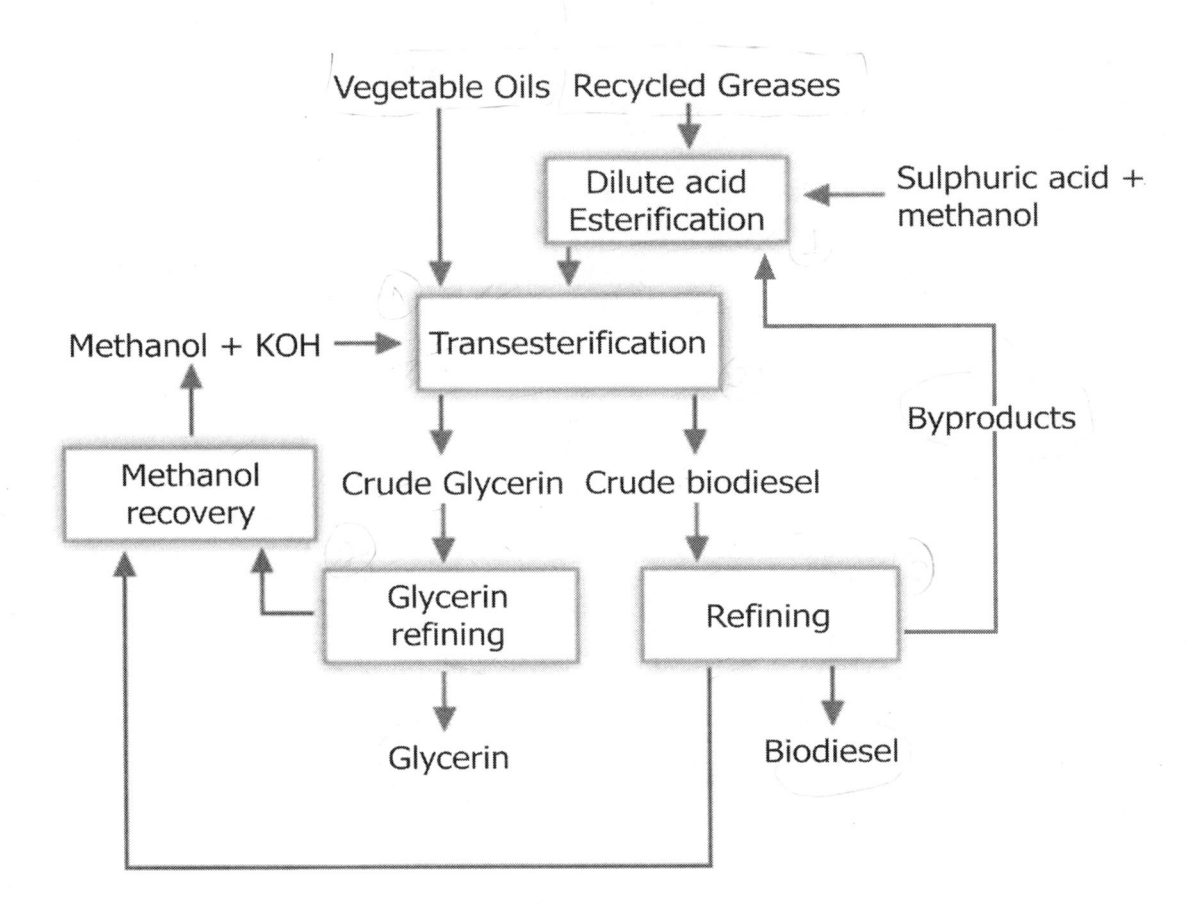

```
                    Vegetable Oils   Recycled Greases
                          |                |
                          |                v
                          |        Dilute acid        <--- Sulphuric acid +
                          |        Esterification           methanol
                          |                |
                          v                v
Methanol + KOH --->  Transesterification
                          |           |
                          v           v                          Byproducts
Methanol          Crude Glycerin   Crude biodiesel                   ^
recovery                |                |                           |
    ^                   v                v                           |
    |              Glycerin           Refining  --------------------->
    |              refining              |
    |                 |                  v
    |                 v               Biodiesel
    |              Glycerin
    |_____|
```

UNIT EIGHT
Cycles

● Definition

A cycle is a series of events, or phenomena, that repeat themselves in the same order until completion. Once completed, the end stage is identical to the first stage, and the same series of events are then repeated in exactly the same order.

In other words, a cycle never stops moving from one stage to the next; going round and round in a never ending circle. The butterfly cycle, (Figure 1), is an excellent example of this. The cycle moves from a butterfly to an egg, to a larva, to a pupa, to another butterfly, to another egg and so on. If the cycle were to stop there would be no more butterflies.

Figure 1

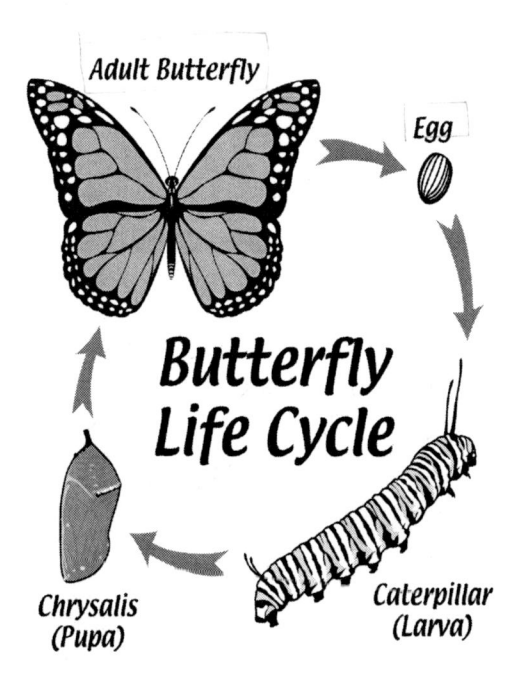

● Introduction

Introductions for cycles are going to follow a similar style to those for processes. They could be written like the following example,

The illustration presented highlights the various stages involved in the butterfly cycle as it changes from an egg to a butterfly.

● General Statement

Cycles, like processes, need no general statement, so move directly onto writing the main body.

● Main Body

You can see that you can follow a very similar style to the one introduced for processes in the previous unit. Look at the following list of important points to note when writing about a cycle.

1	Use a formal style – no direct / indirect reference to people (usually cycles do not involve people)
2	Clearly describe each stage in the cycle
3	Use vocabulary from the diagram but use synonyms whenever possible
4	Use different forms of words taken from the diagram (for example verbs and nouns)
5	Use the simple present verb tense – both active and passive are possible
6	Use time order phrases

If a cycle does directly involve people, as in the case of the life cycle of malaria, it is possible to use phrases like, **if exposed to malaria** and **when bitten by a mosquito**. These phrases result in more formal sentences and avoid the need to refer to people.

● Conclusion

What has already been said for processes remains true for cycles. A conclusion can be part of your essay if you need extra words. A typical conclusion would be like this,

> *All of the stages involved in the cycle of a butterfly have now been completed and another revolution will now begin.*

● Understanding the Diagram

What you have already learned, when studying processes, will help you to develop the necessary skills to write about cycles more quickly.

Again, arrows help to explain both the direction, and the sequence, of events that take place in the cycle. Arrows do not, however, help to explain where the cycle starts. The problem is that if a cycle never stops, how can it really have a beginning and end? This way of thinking is partly true, but it is still possible to choose a more obvious point to start and stop your description of the cycle. In the case of the butterfly cycle, most people pick either the egg, or the butterfly, as the beginning of the first stage. A student starting with the larva or pupa would not impress the examiner.

If this seems confusing, think about writing an essay on the human life cycle and deciding to start with a teenager. Clearly, this is a point that is far into the cycle and should never be picked as the start. If there are lines, but no arrows, connecting one stage to the next, you would usually move in a clockwise direction as you describe each stage of the cycle. Now look at a slightly more complicated diagram of a butterfly cycle, and an example of a main body based on this diagram.

Life Cycle of the Monarch Butterfly

The egg hatches after 4 days into a caterpillar (or larva)

A white egg

To become fully grown takes about 2 weeks. It eats lots of milkweed. The caterpillar has black, orange, cream and yellow stripes.

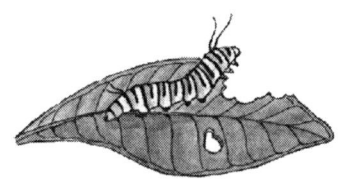

The caterpillar spins a silk pad and attaches itself to a twig. It turns into a pupa with a green outer shell.

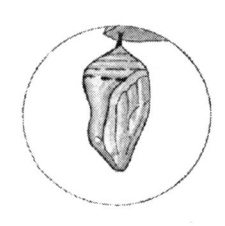

After 2 weeks, the adult butterfly emerges from the pupa.

The adult lives for 2 - 8 weeks. An adult female will lay eggs after mating with an adult male. They are black, orange and white in colour.

During the first stage of the butterfly cycle, a very small caterpillar (or larva) hatches from a white egg after a 4-day incubation period. It has black, yellow, orange and cream stripes and consumes large amounts of food. As a result of this, the caterpillar also grows in size a lot. After a period of time it finds a twig to attach itself to by means of a silk pad. It then becomes a green coloured pupa and stays like this for about two weeks. The pupa then transforms into a butterfly and comes out of it's casing. The adult is black, orange and white. The fully grown butterfly lives for only a brief period of time, up to eight weeks, and must find a mate as soon as possible. Subsequently, a female butterfly will lay eggs that have been fertilised by a male butterfly.

Notice that this essay starts with an egg, and it ends with another egg to complete the cycle. If you start with the egg and end with the butterfly, you have not completed the cycle and, therefore, you have not finished describing the cycle.

Although a lot of information has been given in the diagram, care has been taken not to copy any of the phrases. Copying from the Task 1 introduction, or from the diagram, in any type of Task 1 diagram, will be seen as a problem and will help to lower your grade.

Now look at the main body for the butterfly cycle again, and answer these three questions.

1	Have more active or more passive verb forms been used?
2	Has only the simple present verb tense been used?
3	Is it possible to change all of the verbs used here into the passive form?

A Flexible Writing Style

The passive is often used for processes, cycles and flow charts to create a more academic style of writing. This means that there are no direct or indirect references to people. However, certain diagrams might require the simple present active.

In the case of the main body for the butterfly life cycle, the simple present active is used most of the time. Only the last sentence uses the simple future active (**will lay eggs**) and the present perfect passive (**have been fertilised**).

The passive is not always used here because the cycle describes a living thing, so more direct references to the changes that occur can be made. Also, it is not always possible to use the passive form to describe certain parts of the cycle. For instance, **… a small caterpillar is hatched from an egg …**, **… it is attached to a twig …** and **… as the butterfly is not fed …** suggest that a person is involved with this process.

Other cycles like the water cycle, however, can often allow you to be more flexible when deciding whether to use the active or passive verb. For instance, you could write, **… the wind blows the clouds …** or **… the clouds are blown by the wind ….** when describing one part of the water cycle.

Another example of how flexible this style of writing can be is in the production of sake, a process. It is possible to write, **The sake is pasteurized in order to kill any micro-organisms.** Another way to write this would be, **Any micro-organisms in the sake are killed by pasteurizing it.**

88

Unit 8 – Exercise A Page 132

WRITING TASK 1

You should spend about 20 minutes on this task.

The diagram below shows information about the life cycle of a mosquito.

Summarise the information by selecting and reporting the main features, and make comparisons where relevant.

Write at least 150 words.

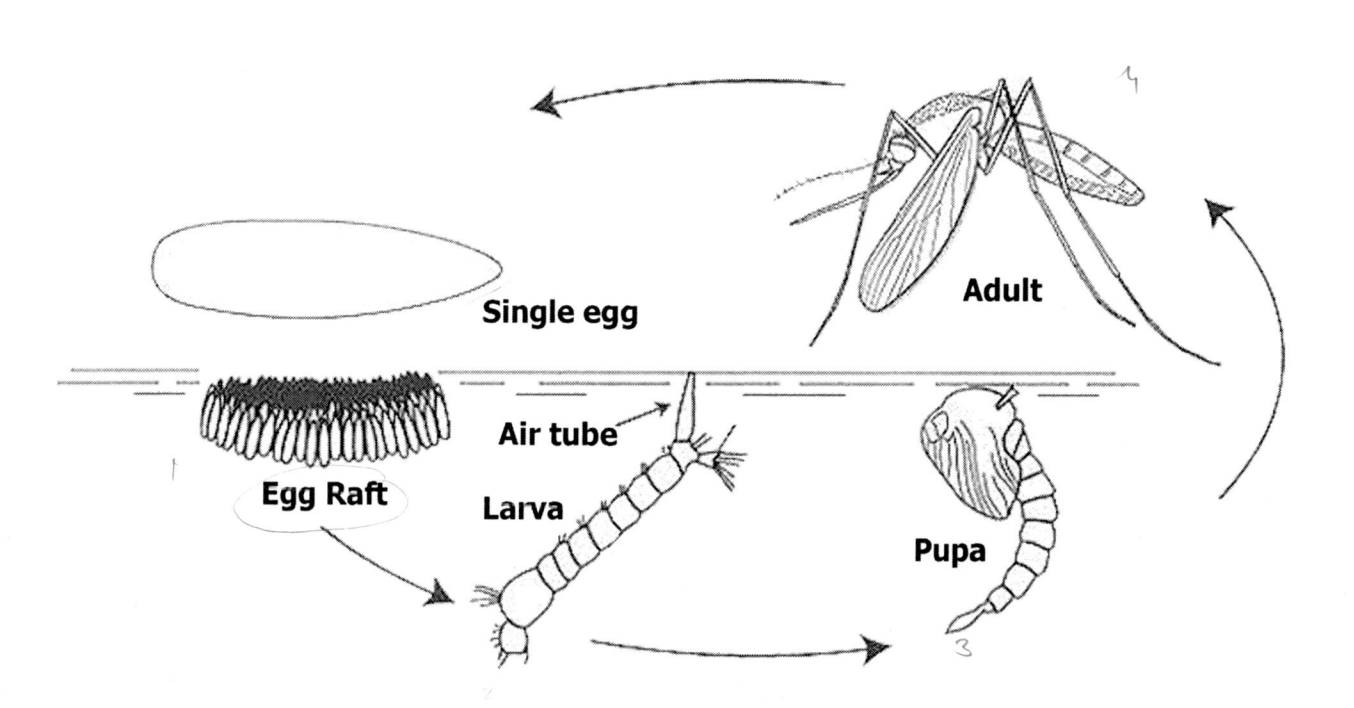

Unit Eight – Exercise B   Page 133

WRITING TASK 1

You should spend about 20 minutes on this task.

The diagram below shows information about the life cycle of a stag beetle.

Summarise the information by selecting and reporting the main features, and make comparisons where relevant.

Write at least 150 words.

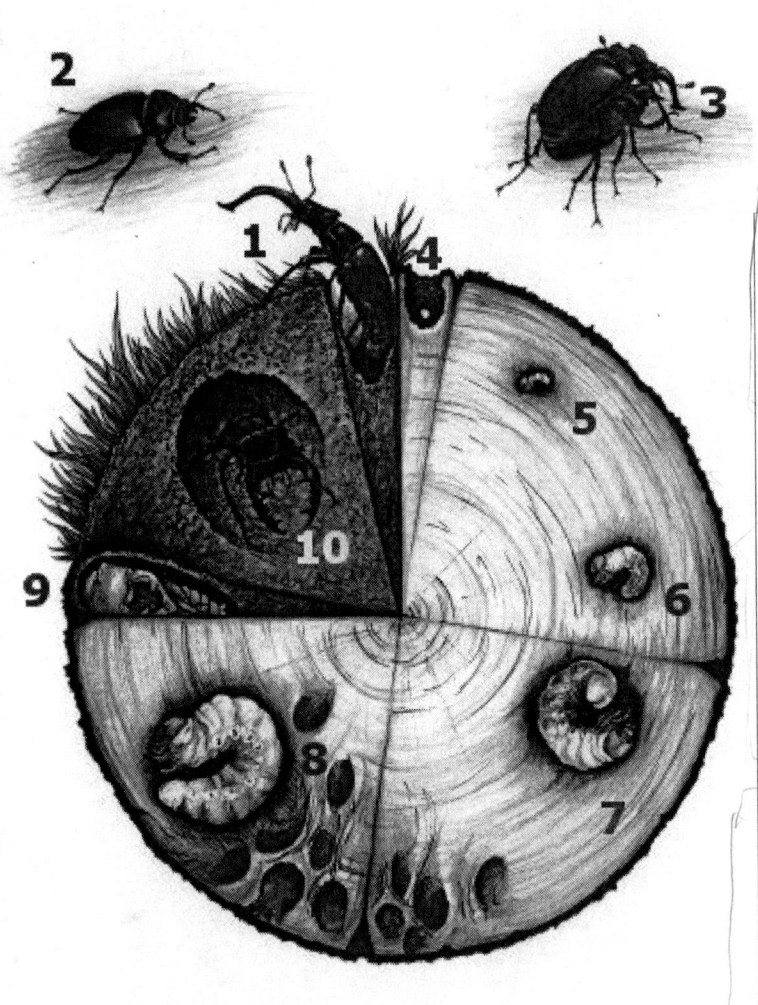

Stage 1 - Male stag beetle looks for mate end of May to beginning of June.

Stage 2 - Female stag beetle is smaller than male.

Stage 3 - Male and female mate.

Stage 4 - Female lays eggs in rotting wood and then dies.

Stage 5 - After 3 weeks, tiny grubs or larvae come out of eggs. Feed on the wood. Cream in colour and blind. Can feed for 3 years or more on rotting wood.

Stage 6 - Larva now has much bigger head and sheds its skin several times.

Stage 7 - Larva has lost its skin again. Even bigger head. About one year old now

Stage 8 - Now about size of adults thumb. Has large reserve of fat under skin. At beginning of summer it leaves the rotting wood. Burrow into soil

Stage 9 - Larva turns into a pupa.

Stage 10 - Fully grown beetle leaves pupa in the following summer.

Unit Eight – Exercise C   Page 133

WRITING TASK 1

You should spend about 20 minutes on this task.

The diagram below shows information about the water cycle.

Summarise the information by selecting and reporting the main features, and make comparisons where relevant.

Write at least 150 words.

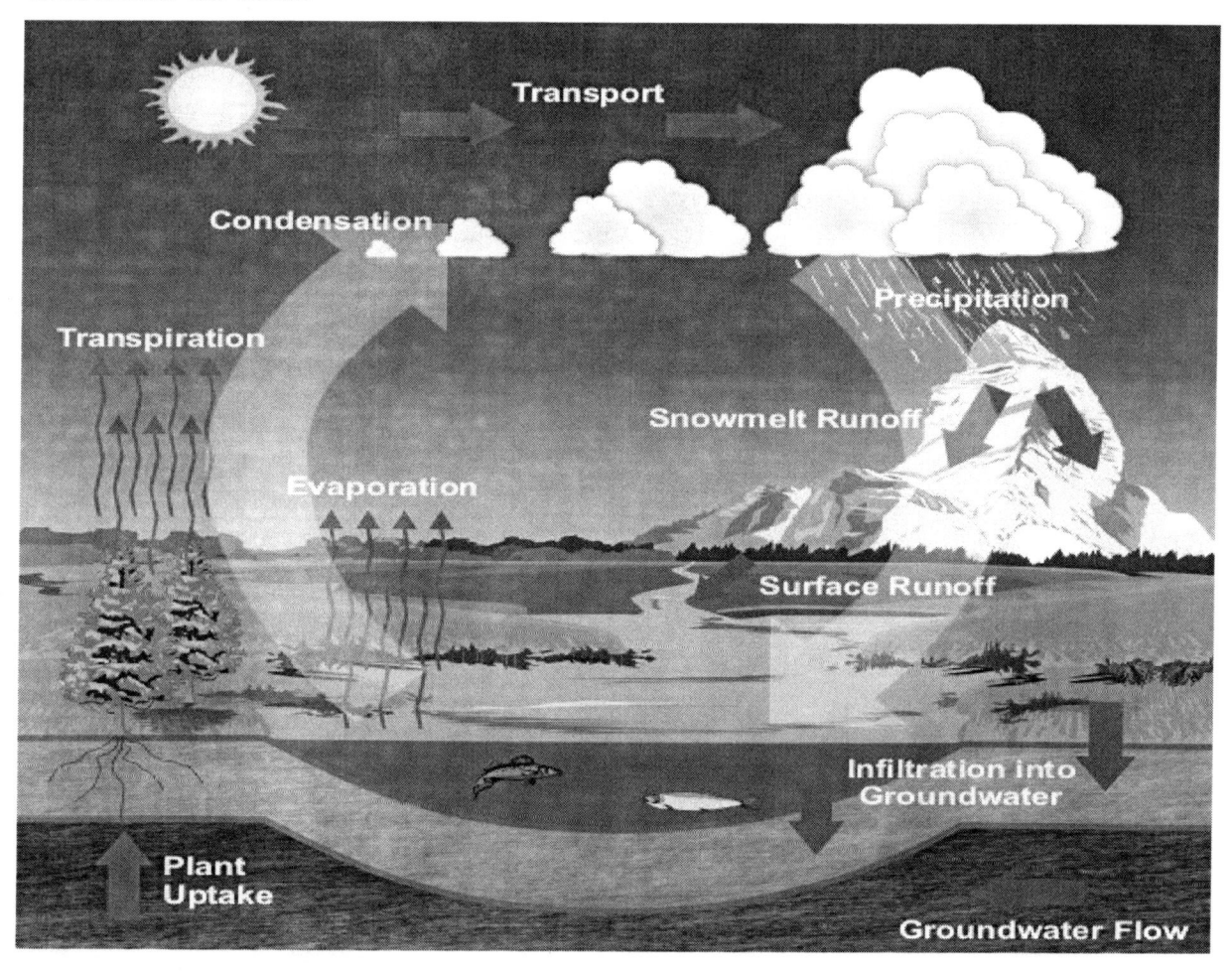

When, for example, describing how rain falls to the earth as part of the water cycle you could state, **After falling onto the ground, the rainwater is then absorbed into the soil and becomes groundwater.** It would not be as effective if less accurate verbs such as, **then runs into** or **then goes into**, were used. Try to select the verbs you use carefully.

Unit Eight – Exercise D   Page 133

WRITING TASK 1

You should spend about 20 minutes on this task.

> *The diagram below shows information about blood circulation.*
>
> *Summarise the information by selecting and reporting the main features, and make comparisons where relevant.*

Write at least 150 words.

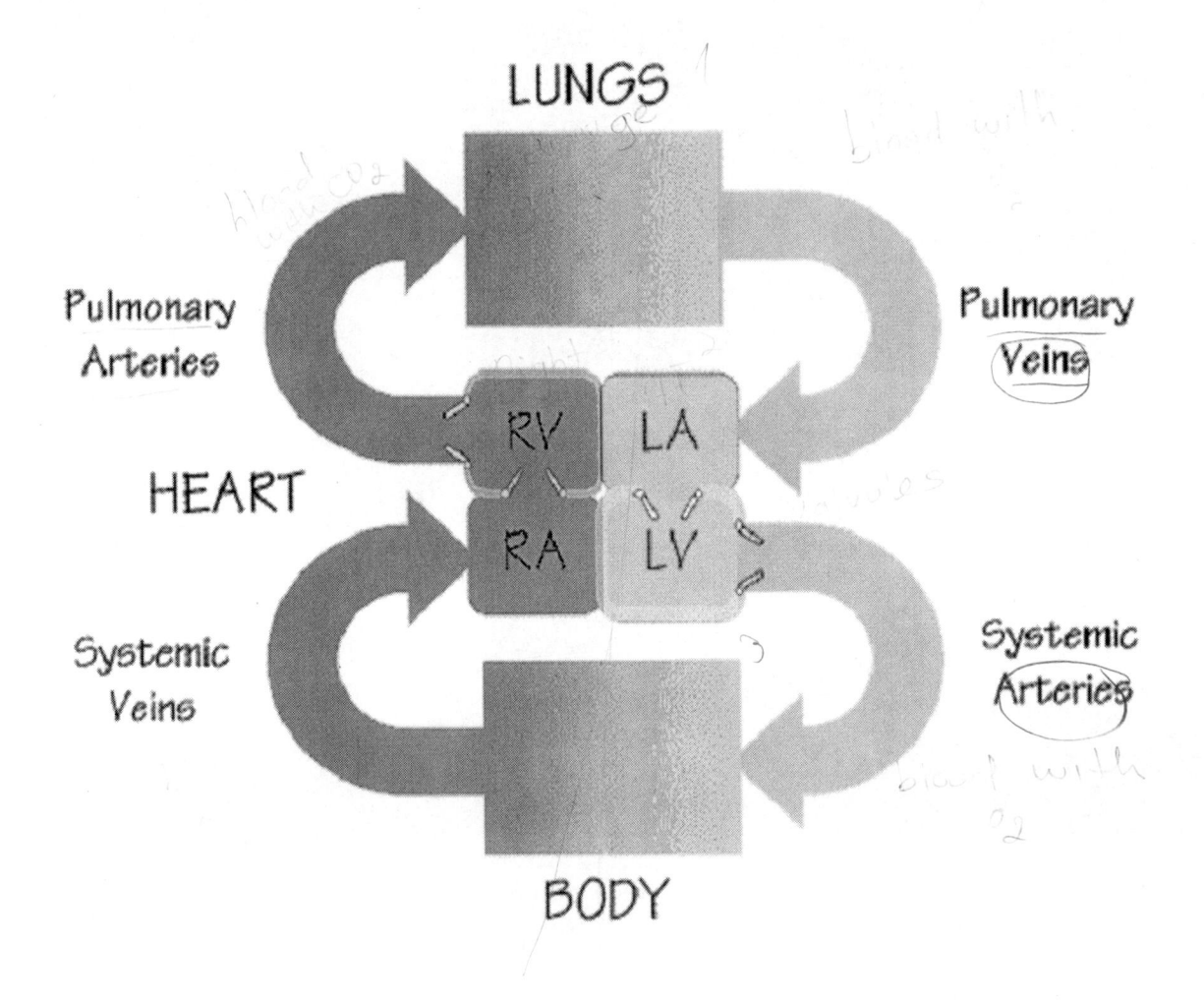

```
                    LUNGS

   Pulmonary                          Pulmonary
   Arteries                             Veins

                  RV │ LA
        HEART    ────┼────
                  RA │ LV

   Systemic                           Systemic
    Veins                              Arteries

                    BODY
```

92

UNIT NINE
Flow Charts

Flow charts have been used since the 1920s. They then became very popular in the 1960s when computer programmers started to use them to map their programs.

Definition

Typically, a flow chart is a step by step analysis of a process often used by some kind of business organisation. This is done to allow a more critical assessment of what happens. Adjustments to the process can then be made in order to make each stage more efficient.

Introduction

As the definition suggests, flow charts are similar to processes and cycles. They usually differ in terms of what they look like and the kind of information shown. The introduction can be written in a very similar style to what you have already learned. A typical example being,

> *The illustration presented highlights the six different stages involved in the addition of a new article to the Wikipedia website.*

General Statement

Like processes and cycles, there is no need to include a general statement.

Main Body

In the diagrams you have studied so far, the focus was usually not on a person's involvement in what is happening. When writing about the production of chocolate, for example, the focus was always on the ingredients used in making chocolate, and no reference to people (direct or indirect) was ever made.

A flow chart, however, very often directly involves people and the decisions they make. It could, for instance, be about how a person chooses what type of transportation to use to go to school, how someone decides whether or not to buy a new lamp, how they determine if a new article can be added to Wikipedia and so on. In each example, the different choices a person makes is a very important part of the flow chart. However, a more academic style of writing should still be written, whenever possible, by using the passive form.

Conclusion

Like processes and cycles, there is no need to include a conclusion.

Understanding the Diagram

Look at the diagram below about adding an article to Wikipedia and the essay based on it. Read the essay on the next page carefully, and try to change it from one that uses direct references to people, to one with no direct or indirect references to people.

Unit Nine – Exercise A　　　　　　　　　　　　　　　　　　　　　　　　Page 134

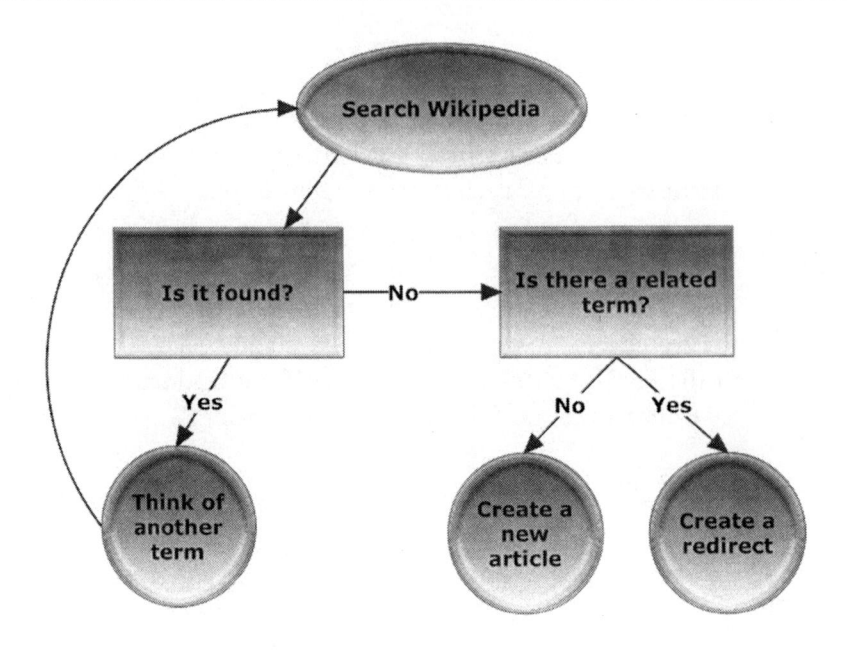

The illustration presented highlights the six different stages involved in the addition of a new article to the Wikipedia website.

Before adding a new article to Wikipedia it is essential for you to do a search using the search engine provided by this website for the topic that is of interest to you. If the search shows that the research term you chose is already there a new article is not needed and so you need to do a new search. If you find no information after this second search when a different term has been selected it is then necessary for you to determine if there is a related term for this. If the answer to your query is in the negative then it is OK for you to write a new article and add it to the Wikipedia website. However, if the answer is positive you can add a redirect for the new term.

Unit Nine – Exercise B   Page 134

Now look at the flow chart about whether or not it is necessary to buy a lamp. Read the essay written for this diagram, and complete the sentences by putting in the correct form of each verb.

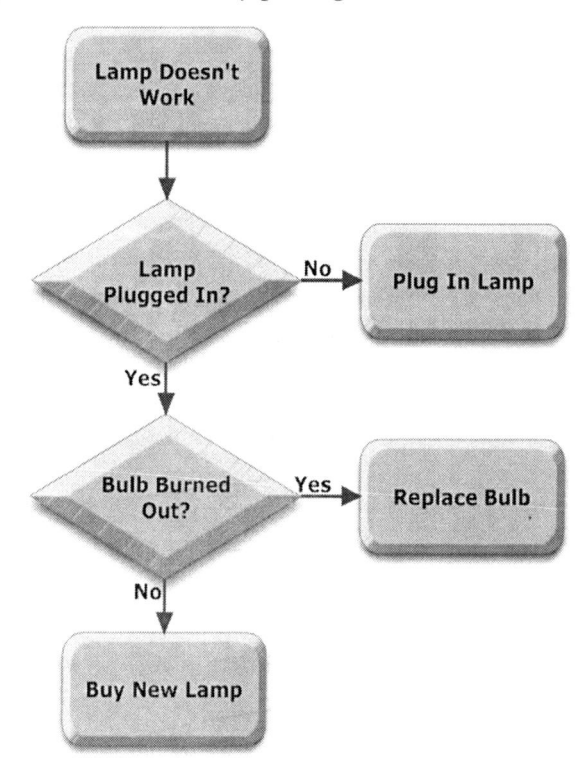

[Flow chart: Lamp Doesn't Work → Lamp Plugged In? — No → Plug In Lamp; Yes → Bulb Burned Out? — Yes → Replace Bulb; No → Buy New Lamp]

The illustration _____ (present) _____ (highlight) the five different stages _____ (involve) in _____ (find) out whether or not it is necessary _____ (purchase) a new lamp after _____ (discover) that it _____ (do) not work.

The first part of this flow chart _____ (start) with the realization that the lamp _____ (do) not work. The first thing _____ (determine) is if the lamp _____ (plug) in. If it _____ (establish) that the plug has not in fact been plugged in then this situation should _____ (rectify). This action _____ (solve) the problem. If, however, the plug has already _____ (plug) in then the bulb must _____ (check) _____ (see) if it _____ (burnt) out. If inspection _____ (show) that this is indeed the case then the old bulb must _____ (replace) with a new bulb. If the bulb is seen _____ (be) still in good condition then it is necessary _____ (buy) a new lamp.

- **Symbols**

When it comes to understanding how arrows are used, flow charts are no different to processes and cycles. They help you to know the order and direction of information, but they are not always used. In this situation, common sense should tell you the correct order of information.

Symbols (different shapes) are also often used. These were originally developed to simplify the interpretation of a flow chart, and to see more easily the transition from one step to the next. Some of the basic symbols used, and what kind of information they contain, can be seen below.

- **Oval**

An oval represents where the flowchart starts and ends.

(START)   (END)

- **Rectangle**

A rectangle is used to show a task, operation or action that needs to be performed.

[FIND CARD]   [GO TO LIBRARY]   [FIND BOOK]   [BOOK SIGNED OUT]

- **Diamond**

A diamond tells you that a decision to a question needs to be made. These are very often **yes** / **no** answers but can be include other information as well.

◇ LIBRARY CARD? ◇

96

When you put these together, you can get a flow chart like the one shown below.

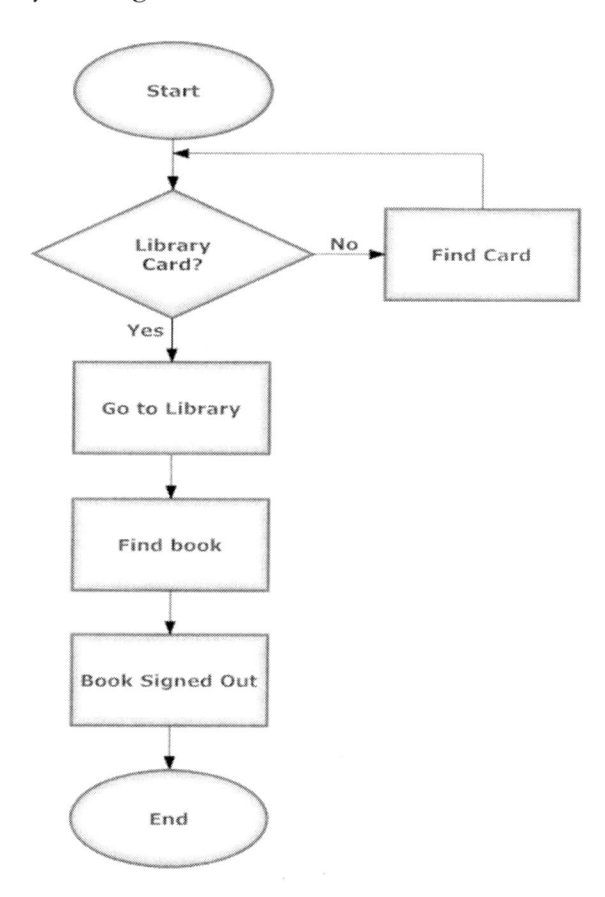

Read the information in each symbol, and take notice of the type of symbols that are used. You can see that we **Start** the whole process with the oval symbol. This then leads to a diamond symbol and the question, do you have a **Library Card?** If the response to this is, **No**, it is necessary to go to the **Find Card** (rectangle). If the answer to the question is, **Yes**, it is possible to **Go to Library** (rectangle). The next rectangle shows that you have to **Find book**. After a suitable book has been found, the final rectangle shows **Book Signed Out** from the library. The last oval is the **End** of the flow chart.

- **Parallelogram**

One other symbol often used is the parallelogram. This indicates input, or output, of data.

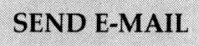

Input data may be something like, receiving a report from a company manager, getting an e-mail or order from a customer and so on. Output data could be writing a report to give to your sales manager, sending an e-mail to a customer, faxing a message and so on.

Unit Nine – Exercise C

Now try to complete the flow chart by using the words from the table. The chart shows two possible ways of getting to school.

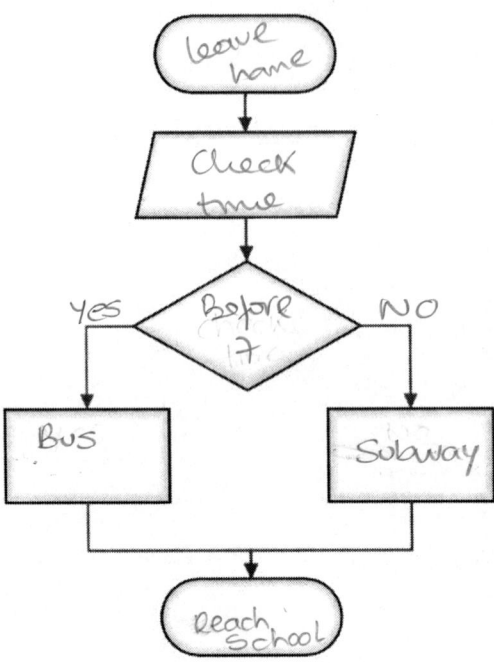

Flow chart (handwritten answers):
- Start: **Leave home**
- Process: **Check time**
- Decision: **Before 7?**
  - Yes → **Bus**
  - No → **Subway**
- End: **Reach School**

Yes	Take Bus
No	Check Time
Before 7am	Take Subway
Reach School	Leave Home

There are many more symbols than the ones shown here, but this is enough to give you some idea of how certain shapes/symbols are used. Although flow charts can be very standard, and might use the symbols originally developed, others can be very different. This can be in terms of how the symbols are used, the type of symbols used and how the data is shown. Any differences you might see, in terms of the style of presentation of a flow chart, does not change the way you interpret it or write about it. Simply decide where the flow chart starts, and work slowly through each step of the diagram.

Unit Nine – Exercise D

WRITING TASK 1

You should spend about 20 minutes on this task.

The diagram below shows how an alarm clock helps you to get out of bed.

Summarise the information by selecting and reporting the main features, and make comparisons where relevant.

Write at least 150 words.

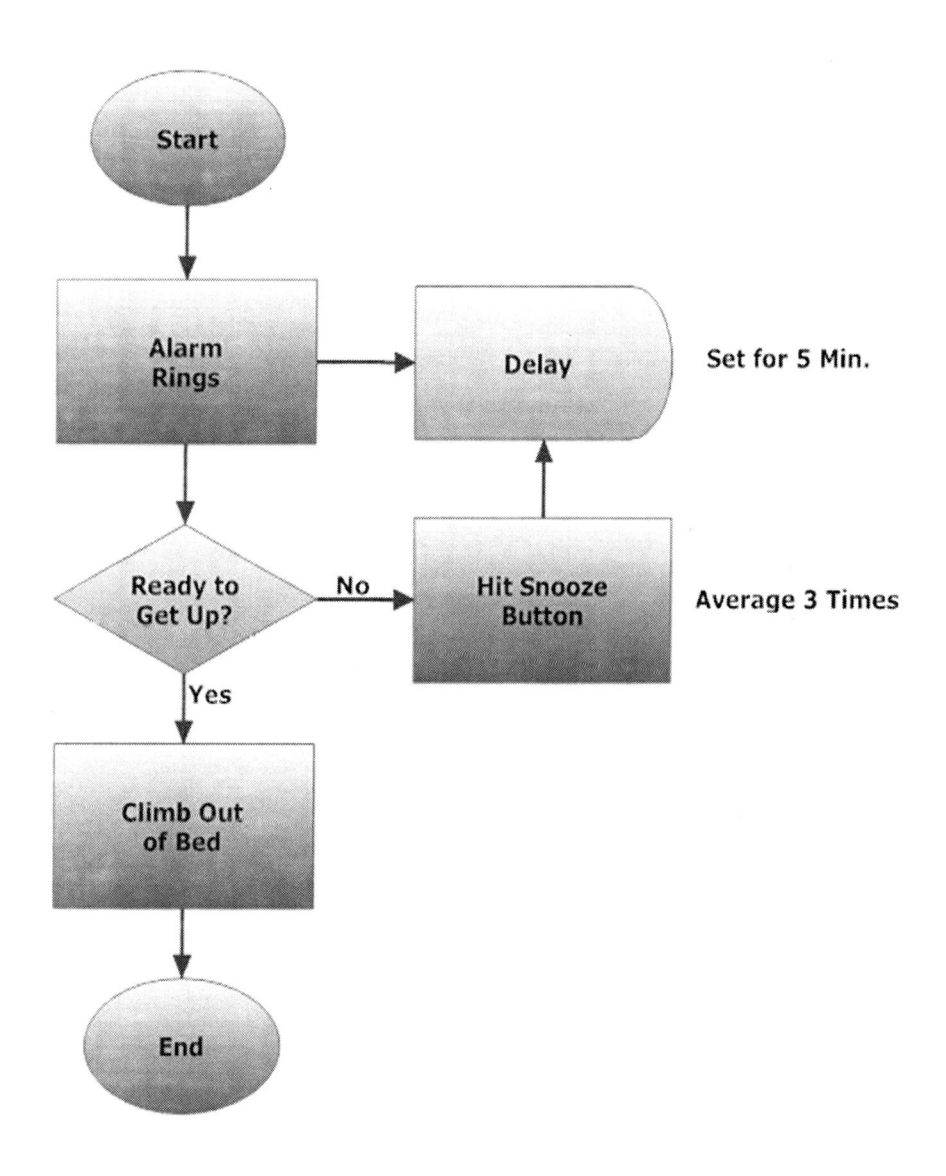

```
                    Start
                      |
                      v
              ┌──────────────┐
              │    Alarm     │─────────►  Delay      Set for 5 Min.
              │    Rings     │              ▲
              └──────────────┘              │
                      │                     │
                      v                     │
                  ╱ Ready to ╲    No   ┌──────────┐
                 ╲  Get Up?  ╱────────►│Hit Snooze│  Average 3 Times
                    ╲    ╱             │  Button  │
                      │                └──────────┘
                      │ Yes
                      v
              ┌──────────────┐
              │  Climb Out   │
              │   of Bed     │
              └──────────────┘
                      │
                      v
                     End
```

Unit Nine – Exercise E

WRITING TASK 1

You should spend about 20 minutes on this task.

> *The diagram below shows how an employee is hired by a company.*
>
> *Summarise the information by selecting and reporting the main features, and make comparisons where relevant.*

Write at least 150 words.

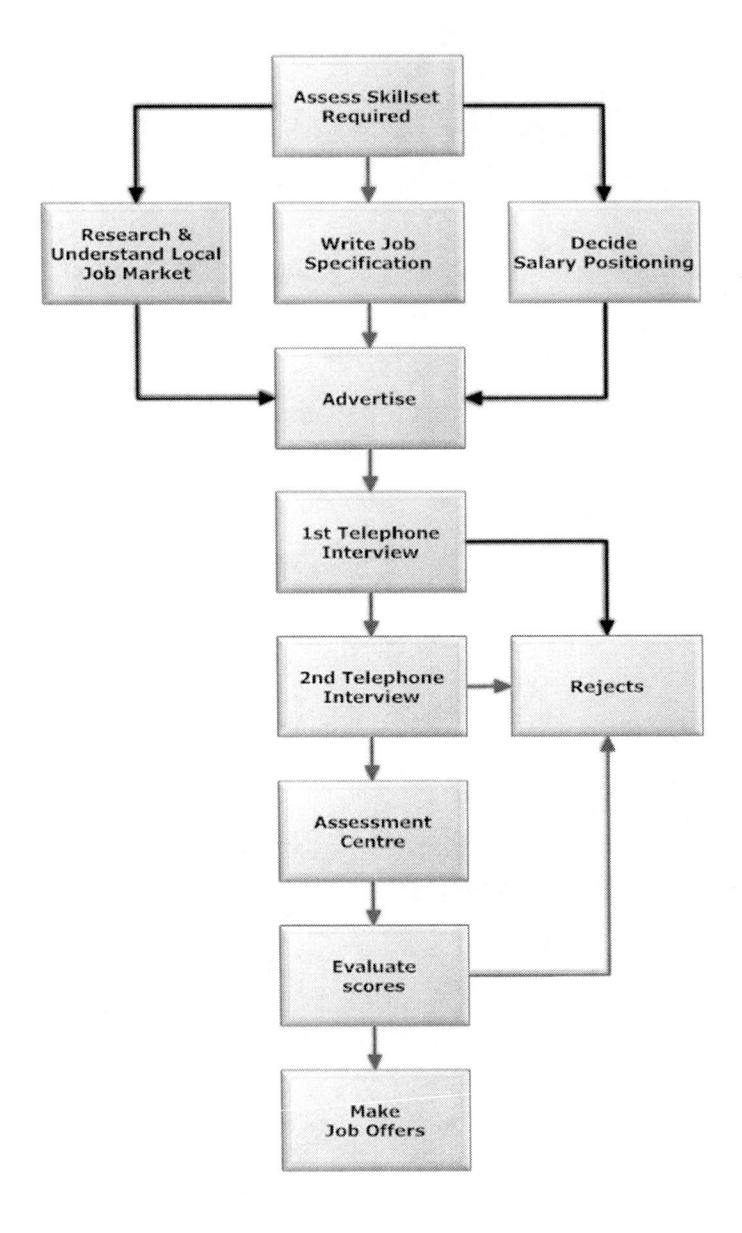

```
                    Assess Skillset
                       Required
                    ↙      ↓      ↘
    Research &       Write Job        Decide
  Understand Local   Specification    Salary Positioning
    Job Market
        ↘            ↓            ↙
                   Advertise
                      ↓
               1st Telephone
                 Interview  ─────────┐
                      ↓               │
               2nd Telephone          │
                 Interview  ──→   Rejects
                      ↓               ↑
               Assessment             │
                 Centre               │
                      ↓               │
                Evaluate  ────────────┘
                 scores
                      ↓
                 Make
               Job Offers
```

WRITING TASK 1

You should spend about 20 minutes on this task.

The diagram below shows the route incoming calls make to an office supply company.

Summarise the information by selecting and reporting the main features, and make comparisons where relevant.

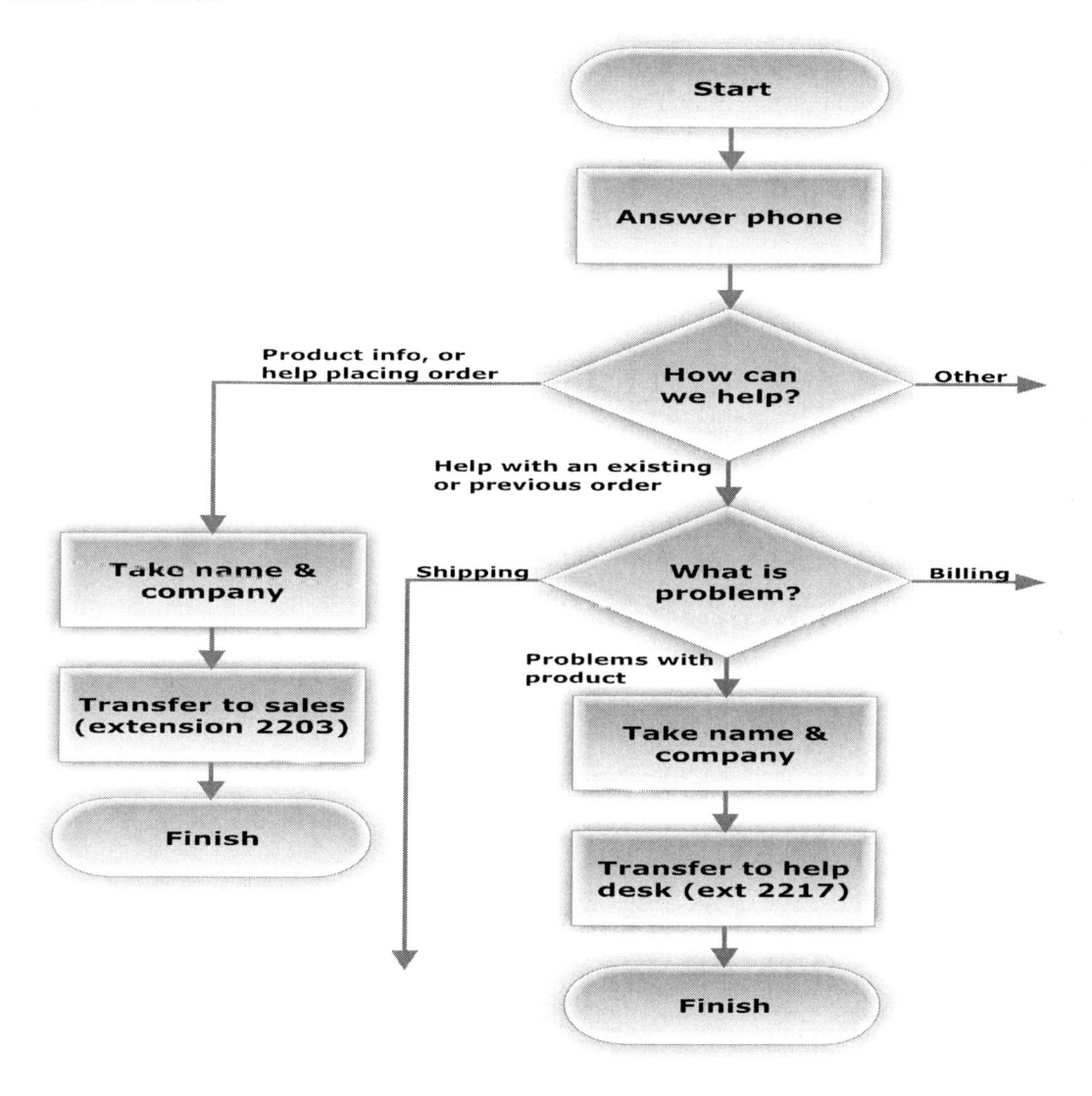

Write at least 150 words.

Summary of Unit Seven, Eight and Nine

Processes / Cycles / Flow Charts

	YOU MUST
1.	try to understand how each stage connects to the next, and describe clearly what happens
2.	try to understand how each stage connects to the next by using the arrows in the diagram
3.	Begin your introduction with a phrase like, The illustration / diagram outlines the different stages in the The illustration / diagram presented highlights the various stages involved in the The illustration / diagram provides information on the different steps in the The illustration / diagram provides a detailed description of the The illustration / diagram presents an overview of the key stages involved in the
4.	choose verbs that are both accurate and more academic
5.	use time order phrases. For example,

Next	Subsequently	Initially	Secondly	When this has been done
Then	After this	At first	Finally	

6.	complete the cycle by going back to the first stage that you write about
7.	try to develop new vocabulary from the words given in the diagram
8.	add a conclusion if your essay is under 150 words. Use the **has been / have been** verb form
9.	use the simple present verb tense – passive form (exceptions are possible)

	YOU MUST NOT
1.	compare and contrast information from the diagram
2.	write a general statement
3.	have any direct reference to people in your essay – **you, they, we, people, I**
4.	use opinions

UNIT TEN

Objects

Another possible diagram is where you have to describe an object or several objects. This could be anything from a building like the Empire State Building in New York, a series of illustrations showing how a particular object has changed over the years (for example, different designs of a computer, tennis racket, car or aeroplane) to a cross-section of something like an ocean.

Introduction

A simple, concise introduction of the diagram, is all that is needed. This will usually explain the purpose of the essay. For example, *The illustration shows the development of a sports car over a 90-year period from 1919 to 2008.* This particular introduction includes a time period, explains that the object to be described is a sports car, and that it has been modified over the years to become a more streamlined, faster vehicle.

Another example could be, *The illustration outlines the main features of an ocean, from above to below the surface, when shown in cross-section.* Here it states that you are going to be describing a cross-section, or slice of an ocean, with many of the important features revealed.

General Statement

A general statement is not usually needed with this type of Task 1. If a particularly obvious overview is possible then put one in.

Main Body

With no general statement needed, the main body needs to be about 130 words in length. This means that you need to describe, compare and contrast as much as possible. If you do not do this, it will be difficult to fulfil the 150-word requirement. No personal opinions must be added. However, if you are told that a building is in Germany, it is perfectly acceptable to refer to it as in Europe. This is not seen as an opinion and may help you to develop your main body more easily. Equally, if one building is made of wood and the other of steel, it is acceptable to state that the former is made of a weaker material.

Conclusion

Again, rather like the general statement, a conclusion is not usually needed with this type of diagram. However, it could be considered if an obvious summary of the object, or objects shown, seems particularly important. Remember, it is not necessary to put in both a general statement and conclusion in any Task 1 essay. You can either include a general statement or conclusion but not both.

Unit Ten – Exercise A

WRITING TASK 1

You should spend about 20 minutes on this task.

> *The diagram below shows information about the bar code.*
>
> *Summarise the information by selecting and reporting the main features, and make comparisons where relevant.*

Write at least 150 words.

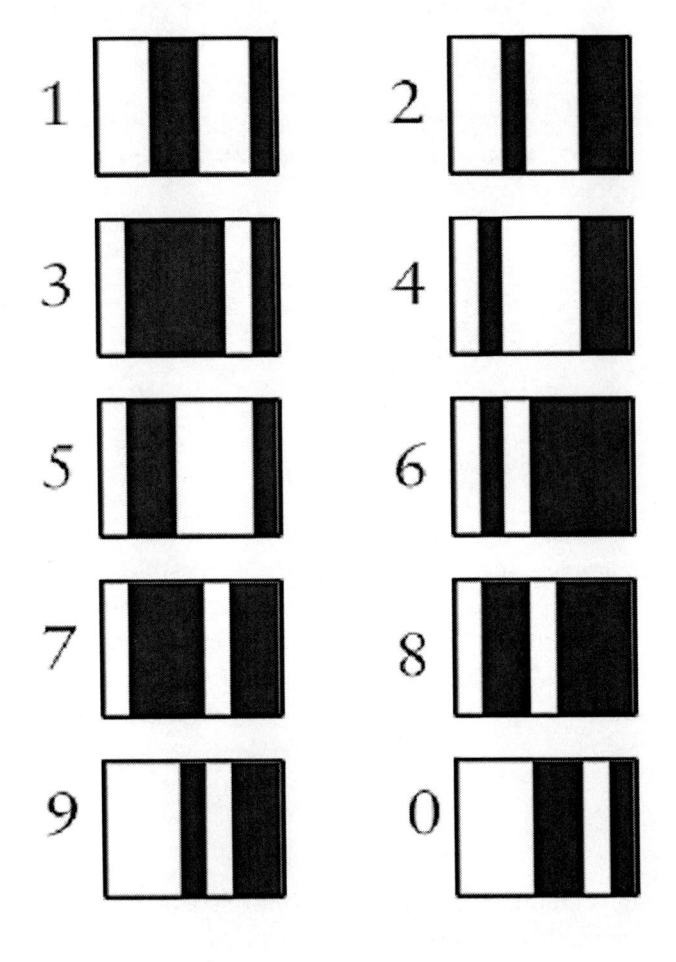

Unit Ten – Exercise B   Page 136

WRITING TASK 1

You should spend about 20 minutes on this task.

The diagram below shows information about the Eiffel Tower and Petronas Towers.

Summarise the information by selecting and reporting the main features, and make comparisons where relevant.

Write at least 150 words.

	Eiffel Tower	**Petronas Towers**
Location	France	Malaysia
Time taken to complete	1889 – the world's tallest	1998 – the world's tallest
Construction Time	2 years	4 years
Cost	$1.5 million	$1.6 billion
Height	986 feet	1,483 feet
Floors	3	88 – sky bridge on 42nd floor connects the 2 towers.
Building Material	wrought iron	concrete, steel, aluminium, glass
Weight	10,000 tons	300,000 tons
No. of lifts	2	78
World's Tallest Building	1889 – 1930	1998 – 2004

105

WRITING TASK 1

You should spend about 20 minutes on this task.

The diagram below shows information about the Solar System.

Summarise the information by selecting and reporting the main features, and make comparisons where relevant.

Write at least 150 words.

Planet	Distance from Sun (in millions of miles)	Diameter (in miles)	Atmosphere	Average Atmospheric Temperature (in degrees C)	Number of Moons
Mercury	36	3,030	Hydrogen Helium	167	None
Venus	67	7,523	Carbon Dioxide Hydrogen	464	None
Earth	93	7,926	Nitrogen Oxygen	15	1
Mars	142	4,222	Carbon Dioxide Nitrogen / Argon	Minus 63	2
Jupiter	483	88,846	Hydrogen Helium / Methane	Minus 153	28
Saturn	888	74,898	Hydrogen Helium / Methane	Minus 184	30
Uranus	1,784	31,763	Hydrogen Helium / Methane	Minus 214	21
Neptune	2,794	30,755	Hydrogen Helium / Methane	Minus 223	8
Pluto	3,647	1,485	Methane Nitrogen	Minus 223	1

Unit Ten – Exercise D   Page 137

WRITING TASK 1

You should spend about 20 minutes on this task.

The diagram below shows information about the world's biggest earthquakes.

Summarise the information by selecting and reporting the main features, and make comparisons where relevant.

Write at least 150 words.

	Magnitude	Date	Year	Location
1	9.5	May 22	1960	Southern Chile
2	9.2	March 27	1964	Prince William Sound, Alaska
3	9.1	December 26	2004	Coast of Sumatra, Indonesia
4	9.0	November 5	1952	Kamchatka, East Russia
5	8.8	February 27	2010	Chile
6	8.8	January 31	1906	Coast of Ecuador
7	8.7	February 3	1965	Rat Islands, Alaska
8	8.6	March 28	2005	Northern Sumatra, Indonesia
9	8.6	August 15	1950	Assam / Tibet
10	8.6	March 9	1957	Adreanof Islands, Alaska

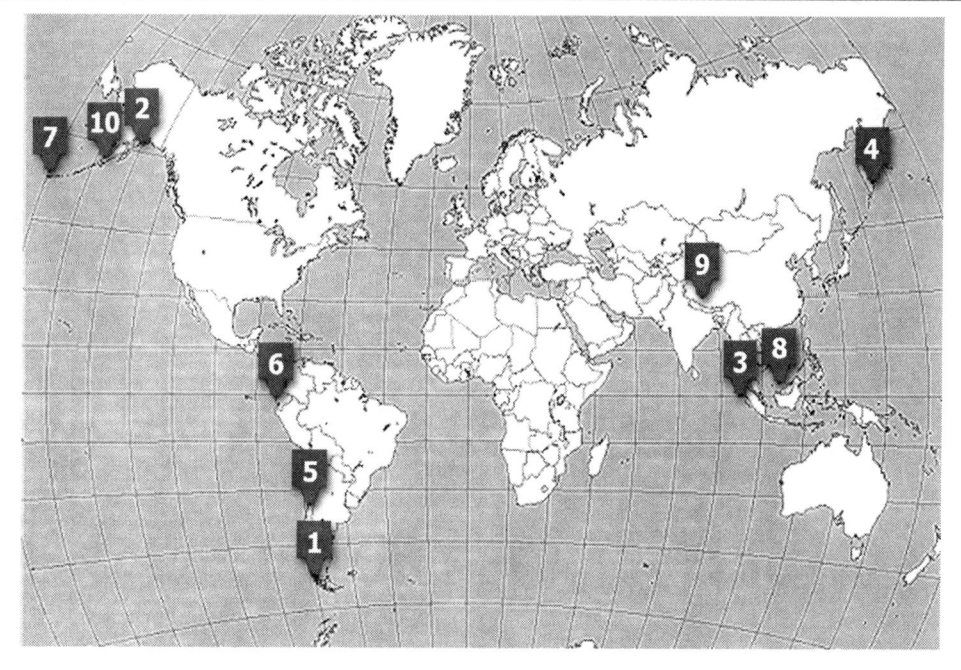

107

Unit Ten – Exercise E Page 137

WRITING TASK 1

You should spend about 20 minutes on this task.

The diagram below shows information about an air conditioner.

Summarise the information by selecting and reporting the main features, and make comparisons where relevant.

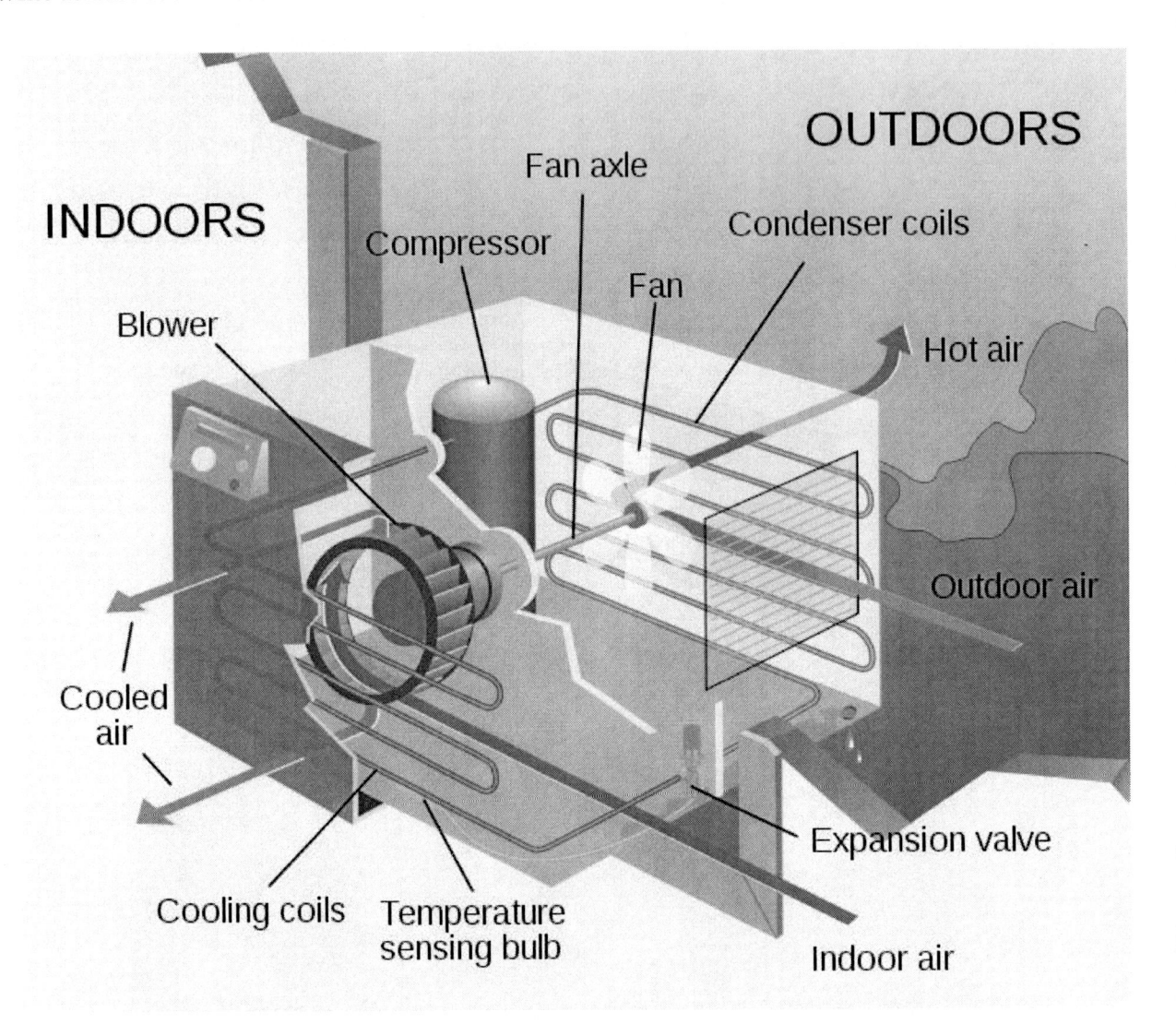

Write at least 150 words.

UNIT ELEVEN
Maps

Introduction

There are two types of map that you might see. The first shows the changes that have occurred, over a period of time, to a specific place or area. The introduction can include the time period and a general statement. Look at the following example,

The illustration presented highlights the changes that occurred in Port Isaac from a sleepy fishing village to a large town with better infrastructure and facilities over an 80-year period from 1918 to 1998.

General Statement

Unit Eleven – Exercise A Page 137

Look at the introduction again, and decide which part is the general statement. As the tendency is for an area to become larger and more developed, typical phrases to use as a general statement of what has happened to the area are shown below.

1. a more residential area
2. a less rural area
3. an area with a better integration of facilities and transportation routes
4. a hotel beach resort with additional car park facilities
5. a town with better infrastructure

Verb Selection

As with many of the diagrams seen in the second part of this book, verb selection is a particularly essential part of writing a successful Task 1 essay. Look at Example B, and decide which verbs go with which item. It might be possible to use some of the verbs with more than one item. If you do not know all of the verbs used here, this is another opportunity to further develop your vocabulary.

Unit Eleven – Exercise B Page 137

a building	a business	a road	a forest

demolish	construct	convert	raze	fell
establish	develop	log	knock down	close	build	widen
	open	chop down	erect	replace	

Unit Eleven – Exercise C   Page 138

As you have seen already in previous types of Task 1 exercises, the use of the passive is a very important part of writing in a more formal, academic style. This involves being able to change the infinitive form of the verb (**to demolish**) into the passive form (**is / are demolished**). Maps often involve changes over a period of time and so you would use the passive form of the simple past.

<u>was / were verb + ed</u>

Now turn all of these verbs into the <u>passive</u> form. Remember that not all verbs are regular.

verb	passive	verb	passive	verb	passive
demolish	was demolished	develop	developed	open	opened
construct	was constructed	log	logged	chop down	chopped down
convert	converted	knock down	knocked down	erect	erected
raze	was razed	close	closed	replace	replaced
fell	felled	build	built		
establish	were	widen	widened		

- **Main Body**

Unit Eleven – Exercise D   Page 138

Look at the following sentences taken from a typical main body. They describe changes that have taken place to a small fishing village. Try to decide how you can improve each sentence. Use your imagination and the ideas given in this section to help you.

1. *The original footpath was straightened and then made into a road.*
2. *The car park was closed to make room for a skating rink.*
3. *The old manor house was converted into a hotel with a swimming pool.*
4. *A few of the old trees were cut down in order to make way for a park bench.*
5. *Before a new fish market could be built the old one was pulled down.*

The key point to consider is that, when writing about various features on a map, it is important to also state their position relative to other features on the map. For instance, many maps will tell you where north is, and this can be used as a reference point:

To the west of ..... / to the left of	To the south of ..... / below the .....
To the north of ...... / above the	To the east of ..... / to the right of .....

If the map does not tell you where north is, standard convention allows you to assume that north is at the top of the diagram. You can also use prepositions to indicate where certain things are.

Unit Eleven – Exercise E   Page 138

Look at the maps below showing how the town of Harborne changes from 1936 to 2007, and summarise the information by selecting and reporting the main features. Make comparisons where relevant.

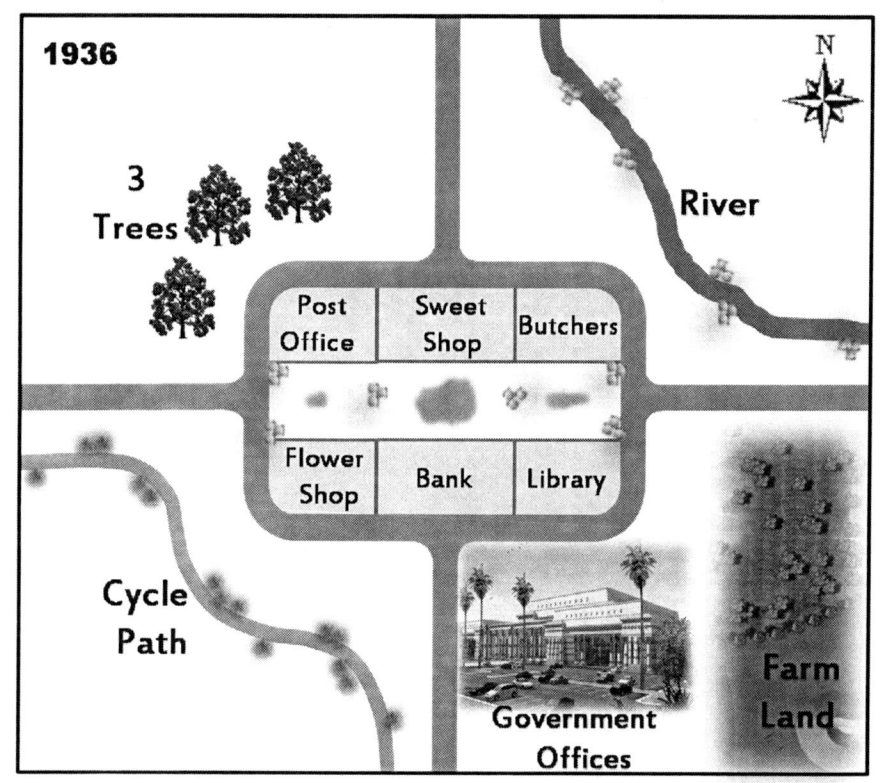

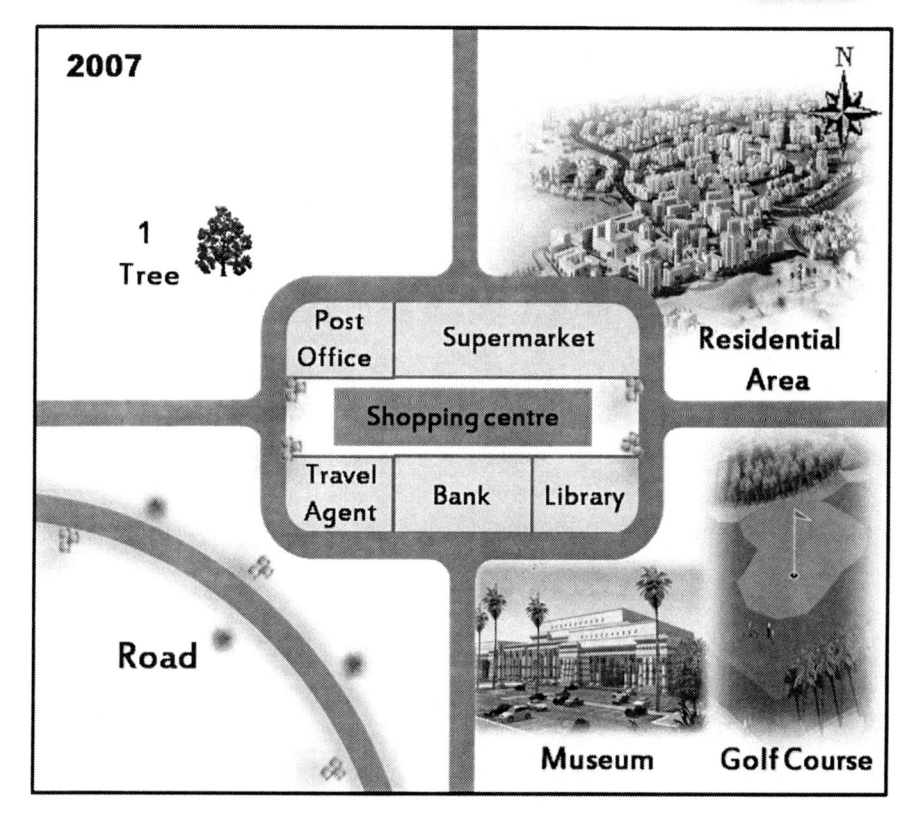

1936

- 3 Trees
- River
- Post Office | Sweet Shop | Butchers
- Flower Shop | Bank | Library
- Cycle Path
- Government Offices
- Farm Land

2007

- 1 Tree
- Post Office | Supermarket
- Shopping centre
- Travel Agent | Bank | Library
- Residential Area
- Road
- Museum
- Golf Course

111

The second type of map provides several possible construction sites for something like, a new building (supermarket/school), motorway or airport. You must write about the advantages and disadvantages of each. **This is the only type of Task 1 diagram where you must add your own opinion.**

Remember to use synonyms to reduce the number of times you have to use the words advantage and disadvantage. How many different synonyms can you think of? Complete the table below.

Unit Eleven – Exercise F Page 139

Advantage	Disadvantage

The kind of advantages or disadvantages that you might be able to write about are usually related to the following factors:

1	environmental
2	financial
3	pollution – noise, water, air, land
4	health and safety
5	social
6	convenience
7	inconvenience
8	time
9	ecological

Now look at Example G on the next page. Work with a partner to decide which of the factors listed above (or others) could be used to discuss the advantages and disadvantages of each car park site. Use these ideas to write the essay.

Also, as this is a map, it is important to describe clearly the location of the important places that you refer to.

Unit Eleven – Exercise G   Page 139

WRITING TASK 1

You should spend about 20 minutes on this task.

> *The map below is of the village of Thropmore. A new car park is planned for the village. The map shows three possible sites (1, 2 and 3) for the new car park.*
>
> *Summarise the information by selecting and reporting the main features, and make comparisons where relevant.*

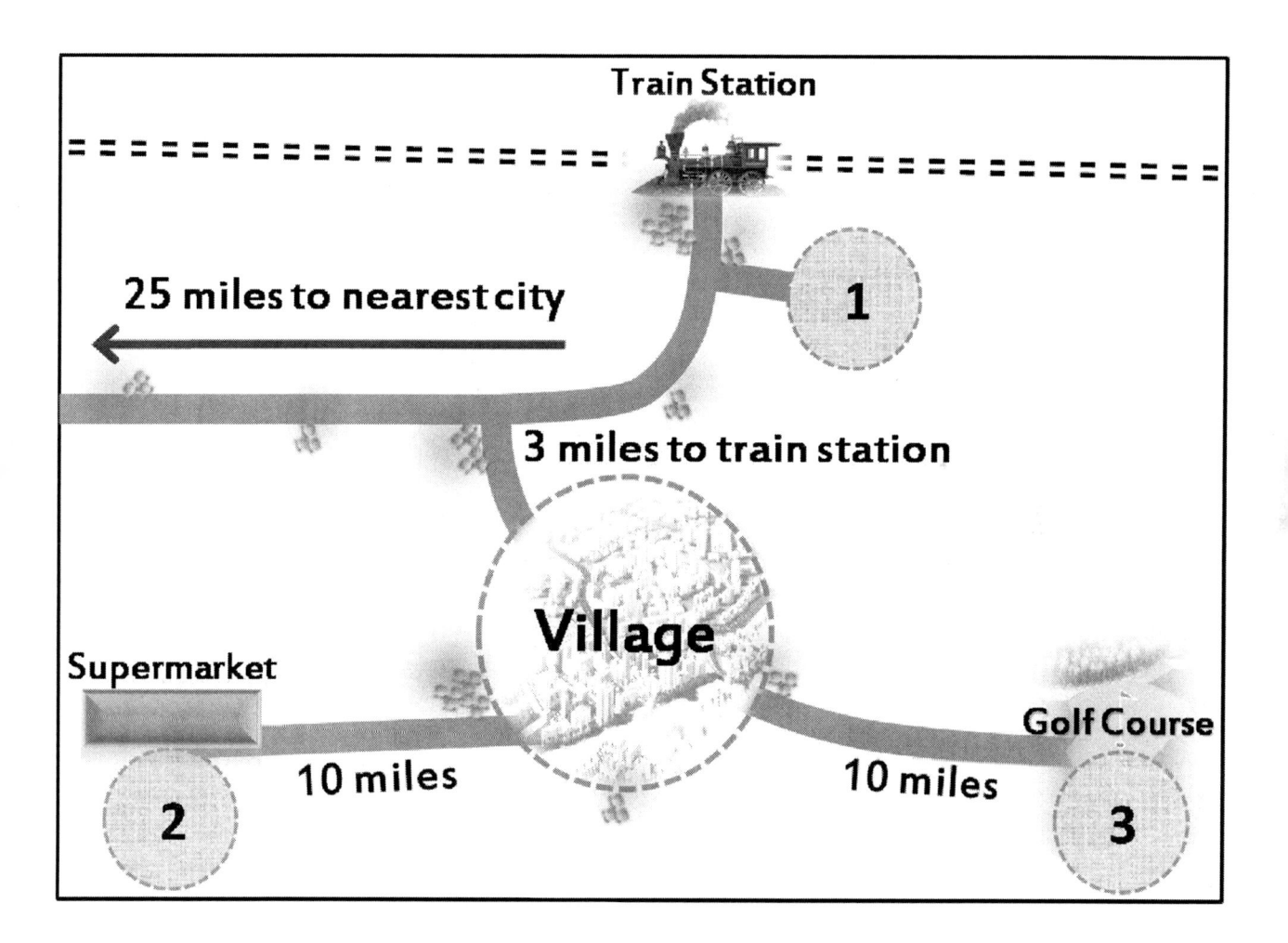

Write at least 150 words.

ANSWERS and Model Essays

UNIT ONE – Writing an Introduction

Unit One - Exercise A

		Extra Information
1	type of chart	bar chart
2	what is being measured	number of students
3	units	1 = one student
4	categories	four schools
5	years	2001 to 2007
6	time period	seven years

Unit One - Exercise B

		Extra Information
1	type of chart	line chart
2	what is being measured	the quarterly revenue
3	units	1 = one billion dollars
4	categories	three technology companies
5	years	2004 to 2006
6	time period	three years

Unit One - Exercise C

		Extra Information
1	type of chart	table
2	what is being measured	sales
3	units	1 = one billion dollars
4	categories	12 cosmetics and toiletries
5	years	2004
6	time period	no time period

Unit One - Exercise D

If you have done this correctly, you will find that you will have the following data,

		Extra Information
1	type of chart	bar chart
2	what is being measured	number of authorised wire taps
3	units	1 = one wire tap
4	categories	two (Federal and State governments)
5	years	1997 to 2007
6	time period	11 years

This new information would enable you to write a sentence like this,

The bar chart shows information about two types of wire tap authorisations over 11 years between 1997 and 2007.

- Using synonyms

Original phrase:

shows information ⟹ compares and contrasts data on the changes in the number of

Original phrase:

wire tap authorisations ⟹ two types/kinds/sorts of wire tapping authorisations

Original phrase:

1997 and 2007 ⟹ over an 11-year period from 1997 to 2007

Having done this, you should be able to write an introduction similar to the following example. Note that the names of the two categories have been included.

The bar chart compares and contrasts data on the changes in the number of wire taps authorized by the federal and state governments over an 11-year period from 1997 to 2007.

- Rearranging the order of information

To make the introduction a little different, you can place the years and time period in a different position. For example, we can also write,

The bar chart compares and contrasts data, <u>over an 11-year period from 1997 to 2007</u>, on the changes in the number of wire taps authorized by the federal and state governments.

Unit One - Exercise E

If you have done this correctly, you will have the following data. This needs to be added to your introduction sentence.

		Extra Information
1	type of chart	pie chart
2	what is being measured	distribution of foreign ladies wear
3	units	percentages
4	categories	seven areas
5	year	2007
6	time period	no time period

This new information would enable you to write a sentence like this,

The pie chart shows information, in percentages, on the distribution of foreign ladies' wear bought from seven areas in New York in 2007.

Care must be taken as this sentence suggests that the clothes are bought from seven different areas in New York and not seven different parts of the world. This basic, revised sentence can be changed by using synonyms and/or rearranging the order of information.

- **Using synonyms**

<u>Original phrase:</u>

shows information ⇒ **compares and contrasts data on the differences in sales of**

There is no time period so you cannot write about **changes in**. However, you can write **differences in**.

<u>Original phrase:</u>

the distribution of foreign ladies' wear ⇒ **clothes for women**

<u>Original phrase:</u>

seven areas ⇒ **seven distinct areas/regions/parts of the world**

As the sentence is not going to be too long, you could include the units by writing, **measured in percentages**. This means that you could end up with a sentence as follows,

The pie chart compares and contrasts data on the differences in the sales of clothes for women in New York, measured in percentages, imported from seven distinct parts of the world in 2007.

UNIT TWO – Writing a General Statement

Unit Two - Exercise A

1. Incorrect

It does not clearly state a trend. Simply stating that something, **rose dramatically** or **fell rapidly,** is not enough as this is too descriptive. You must state which categories fell and which rose. Also, you should never refer to the different categories as, **lines**. It is always necessary to explain what is changing (rising or falling) by referring to what the figures represent. For instance, if you write about a diagram showing the rates of consumption of three types of fast food – **pizzas, hamburgers, fish and chips** – you cannot write,

Generally speaking, while pizzas fell, hamburgers, and fish and chips rose.

Instead you could write,

Generally speaking, while consumption of pizzas fell, figures for hamburgers, and fish and chips rose.

2. Correct

This clearly states not only a trend of movement (in this case sales in all categories rose) but also a trend of quantity (sales in one category – Windows – were **usually higher than the other two**).

3. Incorrect

This general statement does state a trend of movement, but it does this by using the informal expression, **went up**. Never use the words **up** or **down** because they are seen as being too informal.

4. Incorrect

This general statement does state a trend of quantity, but at the end of the sentence the phrase, **over a 3-year period from 2004 to 2006,** is probably repetition of information contained in the introduction. There is no need to state this twice. You could, however, say,

Revenue for Windows was nearly always higher than the other two categories, Google and iPod over the same period of time.

5. Incorrect

It describes what has happened without clearly stating a trend.

6. Correct

This clearly states a trend of movement.

Unit Two - Exercise B

UP		DOWN	
climbed	jumped	declined	fell
developed	maximised	decreased	minimised
enhanced	rose	diminished	plummeted
grew	strengthened	dropped	weakened
increased	surged	dwindled	

Unit Two - Exercise C

The bar chart compares and contrasts data obtained from the Ministry of Defence on the changes in the number of UFOs seen in Great Britain over an 11-year period from 1997 to 2007.

Generally speaking, despite the occurrence of fairly extreme fluctuations in UFO sightings, figures decreased over this time period.

Unit Two - Exercise D

The table compares and contrasts data on the changes in the production of CO_2 in five different countries as a result of the production of energy and their relative ranks over a 21-year period from 1985 to 2005.

In general, CO_2 levels for all countries rose over this time period with the notable exception of Japan which remained the same.

Notice the different way of writing the general statement, ... **levels for all countries rose ... with the notable exception of** ... It would also be possible to say, ... **levels for all countries rose ... apart from** ...

Unit Two - Exercise E

Poland	East Europe	Pakistan	Developing Country
Canada	North America	**Australia**	Developed Country
Japan	Asia	**Egypt**	Developing Country
America	North America	**America**	Developed Country

Unit Two - Exercise F

The pie chart compares and contrasts data on how frequently iPods were used by Australian teenagers per week in 2009 to watch videos.

In general, although the majority of people surveyed did not use an iPod to watch videos, a significant percentage of teenagers frequently used them for this purpose.

Unit Two - Exercise G

One possible general statement is:

In general, the less developed countries eat more unrefined vegetables and also have less heart disease and cancer than the developed countries.

However, in this diagram we can see a very obvious relationship between the two factors. As one decreases, so the other increases. This is referred to as a negative correlation. If one factor increases as the other increases, we could write about a positive correlation. Be careful and not just assume that as one factor changes it has an effect on the other. For example, you can write,

The bar chart compares and contrasts data on the relationship between heart and cancer fatalities and the amount of unrefined vegetables eaten in 12 countries around the world.

In general, there is a very clear negative correlation between the two factors; as people eat more unrefined vegetables the rate of heart disease and cancer incidence falls.

You cannot write:

In general, there is a very clear negative correlation between the two factors; as the rate of heart disease and cancer incidence falls so people eat more unrefined vegetables.

The consumption of more vegetables reduces heart disease <u>NOT</u> people eat more vegetables because they are dying of heart disease.

This might be partly true but would not explain what is a more obvious connection between eating healthy food and a healthy body.

UNIT THREE – Writing the Main Body

Unit Three - Exercise A

1	six hundred	3	18,000	5	1,650 pens
2	3,200	4	2.7 million		

Unit Three - Exercise B

1.	Japan exported five <u>million cars</u> to the US in 1997, the highest figure among all four categories.
2.	The least preferred activity in America was cricket with only <u>6 thousand</u> playing this game at high school.
3.	Online shoppers bought more books (<u>63.7 million</u>) than any other item.
4.	The most expensive four-bedroom houses were in Seattle at an average cost of <u>2.5 million dollars</u>.

Unit Three - Exercise C

1.	Pakistan
2.	Brazil
3.	Literacy is improving
4.	Literacy is generally higher for men than for women
5.	Pakistan
6.	Brazil
7.	Probably if there is an equal number of men and women in the country
8.	It is not possible to answer this question. You do not know the population levels in each country

The bar chart compares and contrasts data on the literacy rates, for both men and women, in six developing countries over an 11-year period from 1990 to 2000.

In general, both men and women experienced increased levels of literacy in this time period.

Unit Three - Exercise D

1.	Turkey	3	Lebanon	5	Algeria	7	Twice as safe
2.	Egypt	4	Lebanon and Syria	6	Egypt		

The two charts provide data on changes in the number of car accidents, over a four-year period from 1997 to 2000, and figures for the number of deaths per 100,000 people in 2000 in eight countries.

In general, the number of road accidents increased in most countries with a higher frequency of deaths in Algeria.

Unit Three - Exercise E

The table compares and contrasts data on the differences in the amount of time spent by both sexes, in an average week in the United Kingdom, on 5 different household activities in 2009.

In general, men spent most of their time maintaining or repairing things whereas women spent the majority of their time cleaning.

Maintenance and repairs (6 hours) was the most popular household task for men whereas it was the least popular activity for women; spending only 30 minutes per week on this. Similarly, women spent the most amount of time on cleaning (16 hours) but men spent none of their time. Men, on average, spent 5 hours gardening which was just over double the time spent on the same activity by women (3 hours). By contrast, the amount of time women spent on cooking (18 hours) is exactly 9 times more than the time spent by men in the kitchen. One further point to note is that women spent the same amount of time shopping as men did gardening (7 hours).

Unit Three - Exercise F

1.	Rises to a peak of 56,000 tons
2.	With a figure of 3,250 kg
3.	Figures increased from 670,000 cars to 823,000
4.	It remained constant at 55
5.	Falling from 65 to 48
6.	Iran and Libya produce equal quantities of oil with slightly less than 70,000 barrels per day per country
7.	People in England spent more on travelling than any other country
8.	The number of migrants increased to over 600,000
9.	One example is Germany, where the number of iPods, at 25 per 100 people, is much lower than the number of mp3 players, at almost 95 per hundred
10.	Italy has the highest figures in both categories
11.	Spending on food increased the most, rising from $85 to $128
12.	Illiteracy is more common among women in most of the countries
13.	A general look at the chart shows distinct changes in levels of tourism with the biggest growth in Japan
14.	The rate of fatalities on the road fell by 15% from 45% to 30%

UNIT FOUR – Analysing Diagrams with a Time Period

Unit Four - Exercise A

1.	e.g. driest month
2.	wettest month
3.	coldest month
4.	constant rainfall
5.	continued increase in rainfall

Unit Four - Exercise B

The line chart compares and contrasts data on the popularity of three boys' names over an 80-year period measured in terms of their frequency per one million babies.

In general, the prominence of two of these names decreased while that of the third rose from the early twentieth century to the start of the 21st.

More specifically, although Brian was the least favoured name in the 1920s with very few people opting for this name, it was then chosen more than the other two names by the 2000s with 4000 boys per million. The only name to experience a continued fall in usage was George, dropping from just over 23,000, the most common name in the 1920s, to a low of approximately 1,500 names: a position shared with Paul. In addition, the rate of parents using the name Paul remained constant at a little over 12,000 throughout the 1950s. One further point to note is that the popularity of Brian reached a peak of 19,000 in the early 1970s.

Unit Four - Exercise C

1.	e.g. biggest increase
2.	smallest increase
3.	two categories the same
4.	comparison of change between two categories
5.	comparison of change between two categories

Unit Four - Exercise D

The bar chart compares and contrasts data on the changes in expenditure on drugs and alcohol over an 18-year period from 1975 to 1992.

In general, more money was spent on alcohol than on drugs over this whole time period.

More specifically, despite obvious fluctuations in sales, the overall increase in sales of alcohol was from $146 billion in 1975 to $148 billion, a rise of $2 billion. In contrast, drug sales rose from $35 billion to $98 billion over the same period of time, slightly less than a 3-fold increase. Both alcohol and drug sales peaked in 1980 with figures of $186 billion and $102 billion respectively, the latter being a little less than the sales of alcohol in 1985 at $104 billion. The biggest difference in sales between alcohol and drugs, in any one year, was in 1977 where sales were $140 billion and $46 billion respectively, a difference of $94 billion.

Unit Four - Exercise E

Note that the use of expressions like, **are expected to, is predicted to** and **is forecast to** help explain that the changes seen in the diagram are uncertain and may or may not happen.

The table compares and contrasts data on the changes that are expected to occur in the dependence of people in 8 different regions on traditional forms of biomass over a 27-year period from 2004-2030.

In general, reliance on biomass is predicted to increase in the majority of these areas with the notable exceptions of China and most of Latin America.

Sub-Saharan Africa is forecast to experience the largest increase, rising from 575 million people using biofuel in 2004 to 720 million in 2030. By contrast, the number of people dependant on this form of energy is predicted to fall the most in China from 480 million to 394 million, a decline of 86 million. The only two areas expected to show no change in biomass usage are the rest of Latin America, from 2004 to 2015, and North Africa, from 2015 to 2030, with 60 million and 5 million users respectively.

Unit Four - Exercise F

Possible answers are:

1.	The biggest overall decrease in preference was <u>walking,</u> falling from a little under 40% to slightly under 10%.
2.	The biggest overall increase in usage was <u>the car,</u> climbing from slightly over 5% in 1950 to a little under 40% in 1990.
3.	The smallest range in type of transport chosen in any one year was 1970 when travelling <u>by bus</u> at exactly 30% and <u>by foot</u> at just over 15%.
4.	Travelling <u>on foot</u> in 1970 (just below 20%) was almost exactly the same as the percentage of people travelling <u>on buses</u> in 1990.

Unit Four - Exercise G

Male	males – men – the opposite sex – the opposite gender – their counterparts
Female	females – women – the opposite sex – the opposite gender – their counterparts

Unit Four – Exercise H

The table compares and contrasts data on six free time pursuits enjoyed by both males and females in three different age groups.

Generally speaking, the trend shows that as both men and women get older they prefer to participate in more solo activities than team sports.

The least preferred activity for males in the 36-45 age group was meditation with 3% participation whereas 12% of all females surveyed did this activity. The biggest overall increase in percentage in any activity for women was for yoga which rose from 7% in the youngest age group to 42% in the oldest age group. The opposite sex, however, experienced the biggest change in fishing from 12% to 45% respectively, a total climb of 33%. No change was seen in jogging at 31% in the two older age groups for women. Similarly, their counterparts saw no variation for meditation which remained at 7% in the same two age groups. It is interesting to note that the biggest difference between the two sexes in any one age group and the same activity was for baseball in the youngest age group; men had 87% whilst the opposite gender had only 2%.

The main body is 149 words in length. Which sentence or sentences would you remove and why? Discuss this with your classmate.

Unit Four - Exercise I

the 21 to 35 age group	the second youngest age group	the 36 to 45 year old men
the youngest age group	the second oldest group	for men who were 66 years old and above
the 21 to 35 year olds	people in the 66 plus group	for women between 46 and 55 years of age

Unit Four - Exercise J

The bar chart compares and contrasts the changes in the amount of television watched per week by men and women from different age groups over a five-year period from 1995 to 1999.

In general, more television is watched by both men and women when 65 years old and above than any other group.

More specifically, both sexes in the oldest group watched a little over 35 hours per week in 1999. By contrast, the 4 to 15-year old girls in 1995 and their 16 to 24-year old counterparts in 1999 watched the least with a little less than 17.5 hours each. The biggest difference between the two sexes in any age group was in the second youngest group where an approximate 17.5 hours was recorded for females and a viewing time of a little over 22.5 hours for the opposite gender in 1999. The only two age groups where both sexes experienced an increase in viewing time were for those viewers between 45 and 54 years of age and those between 55 and 64.

Be careful when using synonyms for people of different ages. For example, if you use the phrase – **young people** – to replace the word – **teenagers** – you have actually widened the definition. Teenagers only refer to people who are between 13-19 years of age but young people is a subjective word that could include people who are much younger than 13 and older than 19.

Unit Four - Exercise K

Diagram One

The line chart compares and contrasts data on the changes in the consumption of pork in America over a 44-year period from 1960 to 2003.

In general, despite some more obvious fluctuations in the amount of pork eaten during the first two decades, consumption remained fairly stable then on.

More specifically, consumption of pork fell to the lowest point over this time period in the mid 1970s having fallen from the highest level of slightly less than 60 pounds per person in 1960 to a little over 40 pounds. One further point is that the amount of pork eaten remained almost constant at around 50 pounds per head from the early 1990s onwards. Two main peaks in consumption for this meat occurred about ten years apart with the first in the early 1970s and the second in the early 1980s when consumption figures were almost identical at approximately 55 pounds and a little under 60 pounds per individual respectively.

Diagram Two

The line chart compares and contrasts data on the changes in the consumption of two types of meat – pork and chicken – in America over a 44-year period from 1960 to 2003.

In general, although the amount of pork eaten surpassed that of chicken in the first two decades, the amount of chicken consumed for the rest of this period of time was always more than pork.

More specifically, consumption of pork fell to the lowest point over this time period in the mid 1970s having fallen from the highest level of slightly less than 60 pounds per person in 1960 to a little over

40 pounds. Although, pork remained the preferred meat from 1960 for a little over twenty years by the 1985 the amount of chicken and pork eaten per person was exactly the same at a little over 50 pounds of meat per head. The biggest difference in consumption between the two white meats occurred in 2003 when slightly less than 80 pounds of chicken was eaten per individual but only a little more than 50 pounds of pork, a difference of about 30 pounds per person.

Diagram Three

The line chart compares and contrasts data on the changes in the consumption of three types of meat, pork, beef, and chicken in America over a 44-year period from 1960 to 2003.

In general, although the amount of beef eaten surpassed that of both pork and chicken in the first three decades, the amount of chicken consumed for the rest of this period of time was always more than the other two categories.

More specifically, while consumption levels of beef peaked in the mid 1970s with just less than 90 pounds of meat consumed, pork fell to its lowest point for this time period with a little over 40 pounds. Despite chicken being the least preferred meat from 1960 to the late 1980s the amount of chicken and pork eaten per person was then a little over 50 pounds of meat per head. Subsequently, chicken then became the most popular type of meat after equalling figures for beef consumption in the mid-1990s with over 65 pounds of both meats eaten per head.

UNIT FIVE – Analysing Diagrams with No Time Period

Unit Five - Exercise A

	Key Features – diagrams with time periods	Can be looked for in a diagram with NO time period (Write YES or NO)
1	The extremes (the biggest and the smallest)	YES
2	The constant (no change)	NO
3	The continued rise / fall over a period of time	NO
4	The only category to always rise	NO
5	The only category to always fall	NO
6	A peak	NO
7	A trough	NO
8	Biggest increase	NO
9	Smallest increase	NO
10	Two categories the same	YES
11	Comparison of change between two categories	NO

Unit Five - Exercise B

The bar chart compares and contrasts data on the different proportions of involvement in the greenhouse effect of four categories of gases.

In general, carbon dioxide contributes to the greenhouse effect far more than the other gases.

More specifically, carbon dioxide is the biggest contributor to enhancing the effect of global warming with a figure of 72%. This contrasts markedly with the category consisting of miscellaneous gases which only adds 1% to this; a difference of exactly 71%. The second main contributor, although with much lower figures than carbon dioxide, is nitrogen dioxide. This contributes to this issue by almost a fifth (19%) and is a share that is nearly three times bigger than methane the third most important category with figures of 7%. The main gas listed here (carbon dioxide) is a little over 10-fold larger in its overall share than the third main gas (methane) with figures of 72% and 7% respectively.

Unit Five - Exercise C

The table compares and contrasts data on the results of a survey to establish the commonly accepted causes of global warming.

In general, the majority of people who were questioned felt that global warming was happening.

More specifically, while almost one in five of those people surveyed (18.4%) felt that global warming was not in fact happening, the majority (77.2%) agreed that it was. Of these particular people, it was felt that global warming was attributable to two main causes; human behaviour and natural climate cycles. The former suggestion was supported by 26.4% of the respondents and was the biggest of the five categories listed. The figure for the latter group was almost the same at just over a quarter (25.6%). Almost exactly the same proportion of people (25.2%) believed this phenomenon to be the result of human activities and natural causes. While most people offered an opinion, 4.4% said that they were not able to explain what the cause was.

Unit Five - Exercise D

1	Just over a **third (35%)** of the people questioned travelled abroad to visit their family or friends.
2	Slightly less than 1 in 10 **(9%)** of those surveyed went abroad to study.
3	While just over a tenth of the people surveyed travelled overseas to get a new job **(12%)**, slightly less than a tenth **(9%)** did so to get married.
4	A little **under two thirds (63%)** of the people questioned travelled for business purposes.
5	**Slightly more than** 1 in 4 **(26%)** moved for medical reasons.
6	While a large percentage of people travelled for these two reasons, it is impossible to answer this question because the percentages in the table add up to more than 100%. This means that more than one reason for travelling overseas has been selected by a lot of the people surveyed. Although the percentages for going on business trips and visiting family or friends add up to 98%, we cannot tell if these are all different people or if some of them are the same.

| 7 | Although the sum of the two percentages adds up to 25%, it is impossible to say if it is a quarter of the total number of people involved in the survey. Some people might have gone overseas for both reasons. |

Unit Five - Exercise E

The table compares and contrasts data on the eight reasons people decided to study a foreign language.

In general, the main reason for learning another language was in order to travel whereas the least important reason was to fulfil the obligations of a business training policy.

More specifically, the main business-related reason for studying a foreign language was to be able to use it on business trips at 36% which is exactly 18% less than those who wished to use it while travelling; the largest personal reason at 54%. The same proportion of people (12%) decided to learn a foreign language in order to either make new friends or because it was their spouses' first language. The third most common reason for taking up a new language was to study abroad at 22%. This was only 4% higher than the fourth reason which was to try and improve their job opportunities.

Unit Five - Exercise F

The bar chart compares and contrasts data on the population levels of 12 aboriginal communities living in urban areas in Canada in 1996.

In general, the 1996 census showed that the largest community of Canadian aborigines is based in Winnipeg whereas the smallest is in Victoria.

The largest aboriginal community (Winnipeg), with a population of slightly less than 46,000 people, is just under 8 times larger than the smallest group which is found in Victoria and has just over 6,000 residents. Toronto and Saskatoon have almost exactly the same number of people in their communities with just over 16,000. Similarly, the second and third largest aboriginal groups are to be found in Edmonton and Vancouver and have almost the same number of people in their groups with a little over 32,000 and 31,000 per community. The combined population of the three largest communities is approximately 110,000 people and almost equal to the combined population of the other nine communities.

Unit Five - Exercise G

The table compares and contrasts data on the differences in the emissions of carbon dioxide by nine private jets, fuel consumption and the hourly cost of flying each jet.

In general, although there is not a perfect correlation between these three categories, a higher fuel cost and, therefore flight cost, usually results in higher production levels of carbon dioxide.

Although the cost per hour of flying time is the same at $6,750, the number of gallons of fuel used per hour for the Challenger 605 is over 200 less than for the Gulfstream III at 280 and 488 gallons respectively. By contrast the Hawker 400XP and 800XP jets both use the same amount of fuel at 188 gallons per hour but the cost of an hour's flight is $2,700 and $4,500 respectively. The two jets most similar in running cost and fuel consumption are the Learjet 60 and the Cessna Citation XLS as they both cost $4,500 per hour and vary by only 5 gallons per hour in fuel consumption.

UNIT SIX – Analysing Multiple Diagrams

Unit Six - Exercise A

The two diagrams compare and contrast data on the preferences, for five types of media and nine activities, of 13 to 17 year olds.

In general, television was voted as providing the best experience while the majority of 13 to 17 year olds watched television and the minority of them read a comic book.

More specifically, television came top in three of the questions posed to the people interviewed. Percentages of 46%, 40% and 42% were given for it being the best media experience, the first to be used and the easiest to use respectively. The radio always received the lowest approval ratings with the notable exception of being the least likely media to be used first which was magazines with only 1% of the votes. While the majority of teenagers surveyed (9 out of 10) watched television, about 7% of them read a comic book. Indeed, reading any kind of material was always a lower priority than listening to music where (in complete contrast to the other survey) just over three-quarters of teens interviewed listened to the radio or CDs.

Unit Six - Exercise B

The table compares and contrasts data on the changes in eight university selection priorities for male and female Taiwanese students considering studying abroad over an 11-year period from 1998 to 2008.

In general, ranking, the cost of accommodation and tuition remained the most important factors in deciding which university to go to for both sexes over this period of time.

More specifically, although university ranking was the most important factor for both males and females in 1998 with 97% and 100% respectively, both sexes focused more on tuition costs in 2008 (97% and 95%). By contrast, teaching quality at 6% was the least important consideration for male students in 2008 whereas their counterparts felt that teaching methods were with only 2% of those surveyed selecting this. The biggest change in opinion for men was the teaching facilities, falling from 66% to 42% but for the opposite gender it was language support with a drop from 39% to 21%.

Unit Six - Exercise C

The two bar charts compare and contrast data on the changes in the amount of land used to grow apricots, prunes and plums in three agricultural regions in Washington State in America over a 14-year period from 1993 to 2006.

In general, land devoted to growing all three kinds of fruit decreased in area with the notable exception of Wenatchee which began to use more land to grow prunes and plums.

More specifically, more land was devoted to growing prunes and plums in Yakima Valley than apricots despite a dramatic fall from a little more than 1400 acres in 1993 to exactly 600 acres in 2006. The only area to experience a peak in land usage was in Wenatchee in 2001 with slightly more than 450 acres being used to grow apricots. The only areas to see no change in the number of acres used to grow fruit were in Wenatchee and other areas where the land used to grow prunes and plums remained the same at almost exactly 100 acres and 70 acres respectively.

Unit Six - Exercise D

The two line charts compare and contrast data on the consumption levels of various types of milk products, fruit and vegetables over a 64-year period from 1942 to 2005.

Generally speaking, while the rate of consumption of most milk categories decreased, figures for fruit juice and fresh fruit rose over this time.

More specifically, despite showing a fall in the amount of litres drunk per week from just over 2 litres to almost exactly 2, the consumption of total milk and cream was always higher than the other milk products. Similarly, the number of grams of fresh vegetables eaten per week fell from exactly 900 grams to a little over 700 grams before consumption levels of fresh fruit surpassed it at the beginning of the 21st century. Although the drinking of skimmed milk only started in 1975, by the mid 1990s it was already the second most popular type of milk with more than 1 litre per day being drunk per person.

Unit Six - Exercise E

The three charts provide detailed information on the top five supermarkets in the United Kingdom in terms of their market share, number of stores and how many employees each company employed in 2003.

In general, Tesco had not only the biggest share of the market than its competitors but it also had more employees.

More specifically, while Tesco captured 26% of the market with only 119 stores to become the largest supermarket employer in the United Kingdom with 200,000 staff, Morrisons only had a 6% share with 46,000 workers employed by them. Both J. Sainsbury and Asda had very similar figures for the number of stores each owned at 463 and 480 respectively with the market share just favouring Asda with 17% of the market. This contrasts markedly with Safeway which had a market share of 10%, a similar number of employees to Asda (92,000 and 117,000 respectively) but had the second lowest number of stores with 258.

UNIT SEVEN – Processes

Unit Seven - Exercise A

The illustration presented highlights the various stages involved in the production of essential oils.

The illustration presented highlights the various stages involved in the purification of water.

Unit Seven - Exercise B

Verbs selected
validate
select
determine

Once a phone number has been selected it is then validated to determine whether it is a valid or invalid number.

Unit Seven - Exercise C

Verbs selected	
order	update
produce	process
generate	send

Both orders and invalid orders are processed to ensure that valid orders are produced. After this the resulting order details generate three specific actions. The shipping documents need to be prepared, the invoice itself, and finally the inventory is updated to ensure that sufficient stock is available for future orders.

Unit Seven - Exercise D

The illustration presented highlights the various stages involved in the production of beer from the original ingredients of malted barley, hops, sugar, yeast and water.

The whole beer production process starts when malted barley is milled before being added to water and then mashed. Following the mashing process it enters the lautering phase which results in malted barley that is then boiled along with hops and sugar. Spent grain is also produced as a by-product which is fed to cattle as feed. Once boiled the material enters a whirlpool and is subsequently cooled before entering a large fermentation tank. It is at this stage that yeast is added to the mix. During this particular stage carbon dioxide is produced and once fermentation is complete the yeast is also discarded. The liquid then enters a maturation phase before being filtered and then bottled, canned or put into tankers for transportation.

In conclusion, beer has been made from the original ingredients of malted barley, hops, sugar, water and yeast.

Although conclusions are not needed for processes, cycles or flow charts, they can be added if the essay is too short with just an introduction and main body.

Unit Seven - Exercise E

The illustration presented highlights the main stages involved in the production of chocolate from four main ingredients.

The manufacturing of chocolate starts with the mixing of cocoa liquor, cocoa butter, milk, sugar and a range of other ingredients. Once these have been thoroughly blended together, the mixture enters the refining stage of production. After this particular stage in the manufacturing process has been completed, it is then followed by conching, a process that results in a mixture called the chocolate couverture. The couverture has to be stored for a period of time before it is tempered. Subsequently, four different and penultimate processes are carried out simultaneously. These are enrobing, panning, moulding and extrusion which then lead to the final stage of this process where the chocolate is put into packaging.

All of the various stages involved in making chocolate have now been completed and chocolate has been made.

Unit Seven - Exercise F

The illustration presented highlights the main stages involved in the production of essential oils from eucalyptus leaves.

The first stage of manufacturing essential oils starts when water is heated in an enclosed container. The steam produced by this action enters a tube positioned at the top the container. From here the steam then goes into another container in which eucalyptus leaves have been placed ready for the extraction of its oils. Following this, essential oils from the leaves and vaporized water move into the topmost part of the second container and then into the next phase of this process. The third container is a coiled tube through which the oils and vaporized water pass. As they do so, cold water is passed through the middle of the coil because this allows the water to condense and some of it then leaves as hot water through a pipe. The water and essential oil then enters a container where it is separated into floral waters and eucalyptus essential oil.

Unit Seven - Exercise G

thermisation / a thermiser / thermised milk	separation / to separate
cooling / a cooler / to cool	standardisation/ a standard / to standardise
pasteurisation / to pasteurise	starter / to start
pre-pressing / to pre-press	microfiltration / a microfilter
bactofugation / a bactofuge	omit / the omittance of

Unit Seven - Exercise H

The illustration presented highlights the main stages involved in the production of two types of Pu'er tea.

The whole process for both types of tea starts with the deactivation of the enzymes in the raw material, the so-called Yunnan big-leaf. Once the enzymes have been deactivated in the leaves, they are then rolled. After this they are left outside in the sun in order that they can be sun-dried. It is at this particular point that steaming and pressing the leaves into shape will result in a type of tea called Sheng Pu´er. However, the other type of tea needs further processing after being sun-dried by entering a post fermentation phase called Qiao Shui Wo Tui in Chinese. The leaves are then subjected to an air drying process which is subsequently followed by the leaves being steamed and pressed into the desired shape. This particular product is known as Shu Pu´er.

Unit Seven - Exercise I

The illustration presented highlights the main stages involved in the production of sake from rice.

The whole process starts when rice polishings are washed and then steeped in water in order to remove any dirt that remains on the rice. Once the rice polishings have been cleaned and spent some time soaking, the rice is steamed. Two distinct process pathways are then followed. The first is when koji is added to one portion of the steamed rice to form rice koji. The other is when sake yeast and water are added to the other portion to produce the fermentation starter called moto. The rice koji and moto are subsequently mixed together where they simultaneously undergo both saccharification and fermentation. After this particular stage has finished, the sake is filtered so that any impurities can be removed. Once filtered, the sake is pasteurized in order to kill any micro-organisms. The sake is then stored and bottled.

Unit Seven - Exercise J

The illustration presented highlights the main stages involved in the production of biodiesel from two main ingredients; vegetable oils and recycled greases.

This process starts when recycled greases are mixed with three key ingredients; sulphuric acid, methanol and biodiesel. This mixture then undergoes a process called dilute acid esterification which enables these products to be transformed chemically. The product from this is then mixed with three other ingredients; vegetable oils, methanol and KOH. Once they have been mixed together transesterification then occurs which results in the production of crude glycerin and crude biodiesel. The crude glycerin is subsequently refined into glycerin as one of the end products of this manufacturing process. The byproducts from the refining of glycerin then enter a methanol recovery stage where the methanol and KOH that are produced are once again fed back into the transesterification process. The crude biodiesel is then refined to produce biodiesel which either reenters the dilute acid esterification process or is used in other ways.

UNIT EIGHT – Cycles

Unit Eight - Exercise A

The illustration presented highlights the various stages involved in the life cycle of a mosquito as it changes from an egg to a fully grown adult.

The life cycle of a mosquito can be divided into two major parts; the part that lives above water and the part that lives below water. The eggs are joined together to form a raft-like structure that floats on the surface of the water. After a period of time, the eggs then hatch to allow the larvae to escape. These live under the water in an upside down position with their tails touching the surface of the water. This allows them to breathe through an air tube. Then the larvae turn into pupae which also live just under the water. Eventually, the pupae transform into fully grown mosquitoes that have wings and are therefore able to fly. They, in turn, will lay eggs that float on top of the water and so begin the next cycle.

Unit Eight - Exercise B

Here you have to be careful because of the amount of information already written about the life cycle of a stage beetle. Any of the information can be used but be careful that you do not copy any of the phrases. Also, remember that information in diagrams may need to be changed grammatically as you write your sentences.

The illustration presented highlights the various stages involved in the life cycle of a stag beetle.

This cycle starts with the male beetle looking for a mate sometime in May or June. Once found he can mate and the female lays her eggs in rotten wood and subsequently dies. Little blind larvae emerge from the eggs three weeks later and begin to eat the rotting wood. This stage can last for three years during which time the larva sheds its skin a number of times. The head of the cream coloured larva becomes very big during this repeated molting phase of the cycle. When it is about the size of an adult thumb and has large amounts of fat deposited under its skin it begins to dig into the earth. Here the larva becomes a pupa which then goes through metamorphosis to produce an adult beetle. This then comes to the surface the next summer in search of a mate.

Unit Eight - Exercise C

The illustration presented highlights the various stages involved in the water cycle.

As heat from the sun's rays begins to warm the earth, water evaporates from the surface of various expanses of water and rises into the air. At the same time, water also enters the atmosphere via transpiration from vegetation that has taken up water through its roots. Through a process called condensation, the vapour released through evaporation and transpiration form clouds. These are then blown by wind and, as they reach high, cooler ground, precipitation occurs and so it begins to rain. Water then falls back to earth with some of it being absorbed by the soil to become groundwater and the rest, along with run-off water from snow that melts, runs into lakes and rivers. Groundwater is able to flow under the ground and can subsequently be used by plants again by them taking it up via their roots.

Unit Eight - Exercise D

Here you have to use two diagrams to write about one cycle. Think carefully about where you start. There are several possible choices.

The illustrations presented highlight the various stages involved in the circulation cycle.

The circulation cycle consists of two main parts. The first is when blood with low levels of oxygen returns to the lungs via the veins and the other when oxygenated blood goes to the various organs of the body through the arteries. To allow blood to circulate around the body, the oxygen depleted blood enters the heart through three main veins. As the blood passes through the left-hand side of the heart, it is then pumped into the lungs through two veins. Once in the lungs, the blood can become rich in oxygen again. The blood, now full of oxygen, re-enters the heart via four arteries. These arteries lead to the right-hand side of the heart from where the heart pumps the blood out through three arteries. These carry the blood to all of the various organs and tissues throughout the body.

UNIT NINE – Flow Charts

Unit Nine - Exercise A

The illustration presented highlights the six different stages involved in the addition of a new article to the Wikipedia website.

Before a new article can be added to Wikipedia it is essential to do a search using the search engine provided by this website for the topic that is of interest. If the search shows that the researched term is already there, a new article is not needed and so a new search can be done. If no information is found after this second search when a different term has been selected, it is then necessary to determine if there is a related term for this. If the answer to this query is in the negative, then it is possible for a new article to be written and so added to the Wikipedia website. However, if the answer is positive a redirect for the new term can be added.

Unit Nine - Exercise B

The illustration presented highlights the five different stages involved in finding out whether or not it is necessary to purchase a new lamp after discovering that it does not work.

The first part of this flow chart starts with the realization that the lamp does not work. The first thing to determine is if the lamp has been plugged in. If it is established that the plug has not in fact been plugged in, then this situation should be rectified. This action will solve the problem. If, however, the plug has already been plugged, in then the bulb must be checked to see if it has burnt out. If inspection shows that this is indeed the case, then the old bulb must be replaced with a new bulb. If the bulb is seen to be still in good condition, then it is necessary to buy a new lamp.

Unit Nine - Exercise C

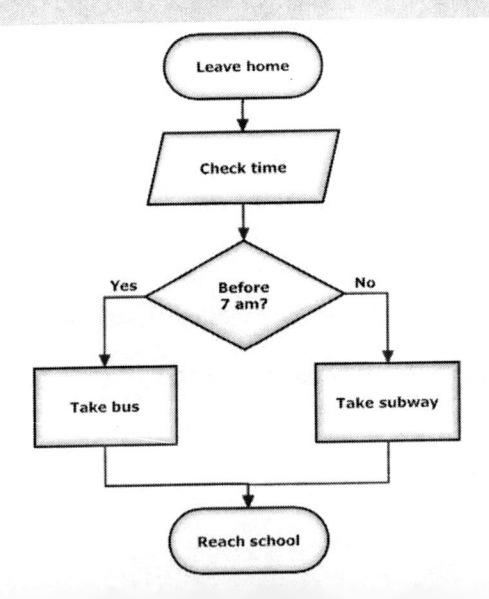

Unit Nine - Exercise D

The illustration presented highlights the seven different stages involved in waking up in the morning when an alarm clock is used.

The flow chart starts when the alarm rings and begins the process of waking the person in bed. If the alarm is loud enough to wake him or her and this person is also willing to get out of bed, then they will climb out of bed. However, if they are not ready to get out of bed, then a snooze button can be hit. If this action happens an average of three times, the pre-set delay ensures that the alarm will ring again after five minutes. This gives the person an extra five minutes in bed before they have to get up. After the allotted time the alarm rings again and the person is again given the chance of either rising or having more time to snooze. If they decide to get up they simply climb out of bed.

Unit Nine - Exercise E

The illustration presented highlights the various stages involved in hiring staff.

The first thing that is needed is for an assessment of what skills the new employee has to have. Then three activities need to be performed before it is possible to advertise the position. Research of the local job market has to be conducted, the specifications of the job need to be determined and a suitable salary also has to be set. Once all of these have been completed, then an advertisement can be placed. This leads to the first round of telephone interviews of potential employees where some interviewees will inevitably be rejected. After this, a second round of telephone interviews is conducted and more callers are rejected. However, the remaining candidates then go to the next stage: the assessment centre where their scores will be evaluated and additional rejections made. Finally, job offers will be made on the strength of the two telephone interviews and the scores.

Unit Nine - Exercise F

The illustration presented highlights the various stages involved when dealing with an incoming phone call to an office supply company.

Initially a phone is answered and the caller offered assistance by asking what help they need. This may lead directly to the request to place an order or for production information. The customer's name and company name are then taken before they are transferred to the sales section on extension 2203. The appropriate help is then given there. Alternatively, the caller may want help with an existing or previous order in which case the problem, possibly a matter of billing or shipping, is ascertained and the required action taken. If, however, the problem is with the product, then company details are taken and the caller transferred to extension 2217 where the customer will be assisted at the help desk.

UNIT TEN – Objects

Unit Ten - Exercise A

Although a bar code seems impossible to read, most people know that it is used to represent various numbers. These numbers go from 0 to 9 and are made up of black and white vertical lines. Each number has the same horizontal space of seven units and four bands. Number one, for instance, is comprised of two units of white, two of black, two of white and then one of black.

The illustrations shown represent the figures 0 to 9 in the form of a bar-code.

All of the figures have several features in common. The first is that they are all of the same width, with a measurement of seven units, and the same height. The second is that they all have four vertical stripes and alternate between white and black starting with white and finishing with black. Six consecutive numbers, 3 to 8 all start with one unit of white whereas only 1, 3, 5 and 0 end with the same single width of black. Only four numbers have a total sum of more units of black than white; 3, 6, 7 and 8. However, black is the only colour to have stripes of four consecutive units and can be seen in numbers 3 and 6. In addition, there are a total of twelve single units of white but only eight of black.

Unit Ten - Exercise B

This type of diagram relies on your ability to describe, compare and contrast information provided. Typical areas to focus on would be height, weight, width, depth, length, thickness, type of material, number of floors, how old it is, size, and how compact, narrow and streamlined it is. If you are not familiar with all of these words, use this as an opportunity to further develop your vocabulary.

The table provides information on the comparisons and contrasts between two famous towers; the Eiffel Tower in France and the Petronas Towers in Malaysia.

The Eiffel Tower is the older of the two and was built over 120 years ago in 1889. The Petronas Towers on the other hand were constructed in 1998. The former took only 2 years to complete, is made of wrought iron and is slightly less than 1000 feet in height but the latter took twice as long, used concrete, steel, aluminium and glass and is just less than 1,500 feet tall. Both of them, however, have been the tallest building in the world with the Eiffel Tower losing the claim in 1930 and the Petronas Towers in 2004. The final cost of each building was $1.5 million for the one in Europe and a little over a thousand times more expensive for the Asian building at $1.6 billion. The Eiffel Tower has only 3 floors and weighs 10,000 tons whereas the Petronas Towers has 88 floors and weighs 300,000 tons.

Unit Ten - Exercise C

Pluto was originally classified as a planet, but it is now considered the largest member of a distinct population called the Kuiper Belt.

The table presented highlights some of the key characteristics of nine planets in the solar system.

While Mercury is the closest planet to the sun with a distance of exactly 36 million miles, Pluto is the furthest, and just over a 100 times further away, at 3,647 million miles. The largest planet, however, is Jupiter with a diameter of 88,846 miles and approximately 14,000 miles bigger than Saturn the next biggest planet. Uranus and Neptune are the closet in size to each other at 31,763 and 30,755 miles respectively. The only planet to have oxygen as part of its atmosphere is the Earth but six planets have hydrogen and 4 planets contain both helium and methane. Saturn has more moons than the other planets with thirty in total whereas only the Earth and Pluto have one moon apiece. Both Neptune and Pluto have exactly the same average temperature of the atmosphere at minus 223 centigrade.

Unit Ten – Exercise D

The table presents detailed information on the ten worst earthquakes in the world. These are spread over a period of a little more than 100 years with the majority of them located in the Americas.

The most powerful earthquake occurred on May 22nd, 1960 in southern Chile and hit with a force of 9.5. North Sumatra, Tibet and the Adreanof Islands all experienced an 8.6 quake and were ranked last in this list. Both the 1950s and 1960s have three quakes each in the top ten list with all of them happening over a 15-year period between 1950 and 1965. Sumatra experienced two earthquakes, ranked third and eighth largest, in 2004 and 2005 with a magnitude of 9.1 and 8.6 respectively. The majority of these ten quakes, six of them, took place in the months of January, February or March. Both Chile and Ecuador experienced an 8.8 quake but these took place 104 years apart.

Unit Ten – Exercise E

The illustration highlights the main features of an air conditioner and is shown in cross section form.

It is divided into two main sections with one half outside the building and the other half inside. The portion outside consists of a compressor, condenser coils and a fan. The fan is attached to a fan axle that connects to a blower in the inside portion of the unit. An expansion valve, temperature sensing bulb and cooling coils are also in this second compartment. As hot air from the room enters the air conditioner, the blower helps to circulate it over the cooling coils. This allows the air to cool and be blown back into the room. Air from outside the building enters the other part of the unit and results in hot air being expelled back into the atmosphere. Water condenses from the moisture in the air and drips from the air conditioner. The temperature of the room is controlled by the temperature sensing bulb.

UNIT ELEVEN – Maps

Unit Eleven - Exercise A

from a sleepy fishing village to a large town with better infrastructure and facilities

Unit Eleven - Exercise B

a building	a business	a road	a forest
demolish	establish	construct	fell
construct	develop	convert	log
convert	close	establish	chop down
raze	build	close	
knock down	open	open	
build	replace	widen	
erect			

137

Unit Eleven - Exercise C

verb	passive	verb	passive	verb	passive
demolish	demolished	develop	developed	open	opened
construct	constructed	log	logged	chop down	chopped down
convert	converted	knock down	knocked down	erect	erected
raze	razed	close	closed	replace	replaced
fell	felled	build	built		
establish	established	widen	widened		

Remember that some verbs cannot take the passive form. Intransitive verbs, such as **become, consist of, happen,** do not take an object and can, therefore, not have a passive form.

Unit Eleven - Exercise D

1	The original footpath, to the left of the ice cream stand, was straightened and made into a road.
2	The car park, to the right of the lighthouse, was closed to make room for a skating rink.
3	The old manor house, situated just below the cliff, was converted into a hotel.
4	A few of the old trees, next to the lighthouse, were cut down in order to make way for a bench.
5	Before a new fish market could be built opposite the pier, the old one was pulled down.

Unit Eleven - Exercise E

The illustrations presented show the changes that took place in Harborne over a 71-year period from 1936 to 2007.

The basic structure of the town is four roads that connect to a central shopping area. In 1936 the north-west quadrant had three trees but by 2007 only one tree remained. Directly below this was a path for cyclists which was then widened into a road. To its right, and across the north-south road were government offices and farm land. These had both gone by the 21st century. The offices had been converted into a museum and a golf course had been established in the place of the farm. The river, which originally existed to the right of the trees, had become a residential area. The post office, bank and library in the central part of the town were left unchanged but the original flower shop closed and was reopened as a travel agent. In addition, the sweet shop and butchers were knocked into one and a supermarket opened in their place. The garden area in the middle became a shopping centre.

Unit Eleven – Exercise F

Advantage	Disadvantage
Benefits	Drawbacks
Pros	Cons
Superior	Restrictions
Dominant	Obstacle
Asset	Inferior
Positive aspect	Negative aspect

Even though these are synonyms – be careful. When using synonyms it is important to remember that different situations may alter which synonyms can be used. For example, it is possible to rent a car or hire a car but you can only hire a person you can not rent them. Also, fruit and vegetables can be ripe and mature but people can only be mature not ripe.

Unit Eleven - Exercise G

The illustration presented shows the village of Thropmore and three proposed locations for a car park.

The first suggestion is to build a car park within easy access of the train station 3 miles north of the village. One of the main benefits of this is that it would allow villagers the chance to drive their car to the station, park and then travel by train to the next town. This would be environmentally more friendly and save time when commuting or shopping. The second possibility is to construct it by the supermarket which is 10 miles to the west of the village. This would encourage people to shop more often at the supermarket and probably save money as a result but this would also have an adverse effect on businesses in the village. The final location is by the golf course and 10 miles to the east of the village. This plan could be seen as rather elitist as not everyone plays golf but might be of commercial benefit to some people in the village if tournaments are held here.